Also by Wendell Berry

FICTION

Fidelity

Hannah Coulter

Jayber Crow

The Memory of Old Jack

Nathan Coulter

A Place on Earth

Remembering

That Distant Land

Watch with Me

The Wild Birds

A World Lost

POETRY

The Broken Ground

Clearing

Collected Poems: 1957–1982

The Country of Marriage

Entries

Farming: A Hand Book

Findings

Given

Openings

A Part

Sabbaths

Sayings and Doings

The Selected Poems of Wendell Berry (1998)

A Timbered Choir

The Wheel

ESSAYS

Another Turn of the Crank

The Art of the Commonplace

Citizenship Papers

A Continuous Harmony

The Gift of Good Land

Harlan Hubbard: Life and Work

The Hidden Wound

Home Economics

Life Is a Miracle

The Long-Legged House

Recollected Essays: 1965–1980

Sex, Economy, Freedom, and Community

Standing by Words

The Unforeseen Wilderness

The Unsettling of America

What Are People For?

The Way *of* Ignorance

AND OTHER ESSAYS BY

Wendell Berry

With Contributions by
Daniel Kemmis and Courtney White

Shoemaker & Hoard

Library of Congress Cataloging-in-Publication Data

Berry, Wendell, 1934–
The way of ignorance / Wendell Berry.
p. cm.
Includes bibliographical references.
ISBN (10) 1-59376-077-9 (alk. paper)
ISBN (13) 978-1-59376-077-9
I. Title.

PS3552.E75W36 2005
814'.54—dc22

2005012294

Jacket and text design by Gopa & Ted2, Inc. • Calligraphy by Christine Colasurdo
Printed in the United States of America

Shoemaker & Hoard • An Imprint of Avalon Publishing Group, Inc.
Distributed by Publishers Group West

The author wishes to thank Terry Cummins, Ernest J. Gaines, and Robert B. Weeden for permission to quote from their work.

Some of the essays in *The Way of Ignorance* were previously published. We thank the editors and publishers of these periodicals and books for their good work:

"Agriculture from the Roots Up"—*Farming*
"The Burden of the Gospels"—*The Christian Century*
"Charlie Fisher"—Originally published as "Trees for my Son and Grandson to Harvest" in *Draft Horse Journal*
"Compromise Hell!"—Originally published as "People can't survive if the land is dead" in *Lexington Herald-Leader* and then, with its present title, in *Orion*
"Contempt for Small Places"—*Farming*
"Imagination in Place"—*Place in American Fiction: Excursions and Explorations*—ed. H. L. Weatherby and George Core. University of Missouri Press.
"Local Knowledge in the Age of Information"—*The Hudson Review*
"The Purpose of a Coherent Community"—*Forum Journal* (National Trust for Historic Preservation
"Quantity vs. Form"—*Southern Arts Journal*
"Renewing Husbandy"—*Crop Science: A Journal Serving the International Community of Crop Scientists*. Reprinted in *Orion*.
"Rugged Individualism"—*Playboy*
"Some Notes for the Kerry Campaign, If Wanted"—*OrionOnline*
"The Way of Ignorance"—*New Letters*
"We Have Begun"—*Slow*

10 9 8 7 6 5 4 3 2 1

"The good, as he came to understand it, is what is uniquely and incomparably appropriate to a given setting. It observes a certain scale, displays a certain proportion. It fits, and the senses can recognize this fit . . . Values, on the other hand, are a universal coin without a proper place or an inherent limit . . . Values undermine the sense of due proportion and substitute an economic calculus. What is good is what is always good; a value prevails only when it outranks a competing value."

FROM DAVID CAYLEY'S INTRODUCTION TO
The Rivers North of the Future: The Testament of Ivan Illich

"Leadership passes into empire; empire begets insolence; insolence brings ruin."

WILLIAM CARLOS WILLIAMS, *Paterson I*

Contents

Part III

Preface

I THINK *The Way of Ignorance* is the right title for this book, but I recognize that it also is risky. Some readers, I am afraid, will conclude from the title that I intend to recommend ignorance or praise it. I intend to do neither.

Some scientists and their gullible followers think that human ignorance is merely an agenda for research. Eventually, they think, we humans will have in hand "the secret of life" or "the secret of the universe," and then all our problems will be solved and all our troubles and sorrows ended.

There are kinds and degrees of ignorance that are remediable, of course, and we have no excuse for not learning all we can. Within limits, we can learn and think; we can read, hear, and see; we can remember. We don't have to live in a world defined by professional and political gibberish.

But the essays and speeches in this book have been written with the understanding, hardly a novelty, that our ignorance ultimately is irremediable, that some problems are unsolvable and some questions unanswerable—that, do what we will, we are never going to be free of mortality, partiality, fallibility, and error. The extent of our knowledge will always be, at the same time, the measure of the extent of our ignorance.

Because ignorance is thus a part of our creaturely definition, we need an appropriate way: a way of ignorance, which is the way of neighborly love, kindness, caution, care, appropriate scale, thrift, good work, right livelihood. Creatures who have armed themselves with the power of limitless destruction should not be following any way laid out by their limited knowledge and their unseemly pride in it.

The way of ignorance, therefore, is to be careful, to know the limits and the efficacy of our knowledge. It is to be humble and to work on an appropriate scale.

------◆------

Some people who have written about my essays have honored me by supposing that I am a philosopher or a scholar. I am neither. I have no talent for the abstract thought of philosophers and not much interest in it. My reading in philosophy is scant and unskilled. And though I have been a constant reader for most of my life, I have never read systematically. I own a fair number of useful books, but I don't live near a good library, and I am in no sense a researcher. For many years, in writing my essays, my "research" has consisted in large part of articles that people have sent to me in the mail. I have tried to be both consistent and honest, aims that sometimes are contradictory, but I have never attempted to contrive a "system" of thought.

And so I hope my readers will recognize what an ad hoc affair my essay writing has been. As a writer on agriculture I have of course been under the influence of other writers, but what I have written has also been influenced immeasurably by the instruction, conversation, and example of farmers I have known, and by my daily work on my own small farm. I am a small writer as I am a small farmer. My work is no more professional than it is official. In my essays I have meant to speak for myself and nobody else. The work that I feel best about I have done as an amateur: for love. But in my essays especially I have been motivated also by fear of our violence to one another and to the world, and by hope that we might do better. If I had not been so reasonably afraid, my essays at least would have been much different and many fewer.

------◆------

One mind alone, like one life alone, is perfectly worthless, not even imaginable.

For many years I have used my brother's thinking as a test of my own, and so I am always indebted to him, even when I have not shown him my drafts or carried them to his house to read them to him. I would not dare to suppose that he and I agree on everything, though we agree on much, but "What would John say?" is always one of my critical questions.

These essays, and especially those in Part II, grow directly out of my long conversation with Wes Jackson. Questions having to do with the limits of human knowledge have occupied us for years, as we have thought both separately and together. As a sort of flat-earther, proud but humble, I am often in need of help from a friendly but critical scientist. Wes has given me such help in generous abundance, and he has saved me from many errors, laughter blessedly a part of the process.

Another constant partner of my thoughts is Tanya Berry, my wife, who has taught me to think twice about a lot of things. She has typed all of these essays, at least once, on our old Royal standard typewriter, which, like ourselves, is still working after long use. "What would Tanya say?" is another of my critical questions, and she still tells me.

A somewhat different Tanya, my friend Tanya Charlton, typed my palimpsest typescripts onto a computer disk, and improved my life by her patience and good humor when I phoned endless corrections at odd hours.

David Charlton and Mark Lawson, ministers, were much in my mind while I was writing "The Burden of the Gospels." By being my friends and by reading critically what I wrote, they helped to steady my thoughts.

Julie Wrinn copyedited this book. A copyeditor, I guess, can get away with being just a regularizer, but Julie is also an encourager and a challenger. She advises, I resist, and then, looking over the precipice of publication, I often change my mind.

Jack Shoemaker and Trish Hoard, incorporated and in person, have given me as before the comfort of knowing that my publishers are my friends and are interested, as friends, in what I write.

Part I

Secrecy vs. Rights

ON JANUARY 12, 2004, according to David Stout of the *New York Times*, the Supreme Court refused to reconsider a lower court's ruling "that the Justice Department was within its rights in refusing to identify more than 700 people, most of those Arabs or Muslims, arrested for immigration violations in connection with the attacks" of September 11, 2001. Mr. Stout usefully reduced the case to its gist by writing that it "pitted two fundamental values against each other—the right of the public to know details of how its government operates and the government's need to keep some information secret to protect national security."

The Supreme Court thus decided, in effect, to support the Justice Department's policy of holding prisoners in secret for the sake of national security, but it did not resolve the conflict between "the right of the public to know" and "the government's need" for secrecy.

The first thing we notice, of course, is that secret imprisonment necessarily denies to the prisoner any semblance of due process. But more is involved than that, and I want to try to say what more is involved.

The rights of the people are openly declared (not granted, but affirmed) in the founding documents of our nation. These rights were not understood as given, and therefore retractable, by the government at its discretion; they were understood, rather, as entitlements originating in "the laws of nature and of nature's God." The government's need for secrecy, by contrast, is a need that can be defined only by the government, and only in secret.

A government's wish to rule in secret on its own initiative and authority is perfectly understandable; this is a merely human weakness. *Of course* government officials would like to keep some information secret for reasons of national security, as well as for many other reasons that may readily be imagined. It is nevertheless true that a government's wish to govern in secret is the same as the wish to govern tyrannically, as we are shown by the secret imprisonment of the seven hundred.

Perhaps it is always the tendency of those in power to wish to rule autocratically, and this is what our founders feared and provided against. Aside from any issue of faith or theory, there is a practical reason for ascribing human rights to "the laws of nature and of nature's God." Rights that originate beyond and above governmental power cannot justly be abridged or revoked by a government.

In the United States the major political dialogue has been about rights: Can the fundamental human rights, set forth in the Declaration of Independence and the Constitution as belonging equally to all, be justifiably withheld from some? Over the course of our history until now, we have decided that they cannot be. We have not decided this without reason. The most persuasive argument of the Civil Rights Movement, for example, was that you cannot withhold civil rights from some people and still confidently guarantee the same rights to others; the denial turned against one group at one time can, at another time, be turned against another group. Injustices condoned against a native racial minority may with the same impunity be used against Arab and Muslim immigrants, or against dissident white protestants. Governments, the Declaration says, derive "their just powers from the consent of the governed." If the governed accept or allow a government that is arbitrary, self-authorized, and self-justified, then, whatever may be the fate of national security, mere citizens will no longer be secure in their rights.

There is no reason, now or ever, to make light of what we are now calling "national security." People want, naturally enough, "to be secure in their persons, houses, papers, and effects," not only against "unreasonable searches and seizures," but also against violence, whether domestic or foreign in origin. That is why we threw off the arbitrary rule of England and instituted a government of our own; we wished to be secure, which is to say that we wished not to be governed except by our own consent.

We may say then that national security has been our concern from the beginning, and that from the beginning the designated purpose of the nation was to secure the rights to which its citizens individually were entitled by the laws of nature and of nature's God. The two kinds of security were understood as one. If the security of the nation ceases to imply the security of all its inhabitants in their God-given rights, then, according to the Declaration of Independence, that nation's government will have delegitimized itself and should be replaced. That is not the wild idea of somebody in the current crop of left-wingers or right-wingers, but merely what the Declaration says, and we have been living with it unobjectingly for going on 228 years.

People's wish to be safe is undoubtedly one of the paramount concerns of politics and government. We want to be safe because we have perceived accurately that we live under threat of many dangers. We expect, rightly, that the government should give us reasonable protections against at least some of those dangers, especially the ones against which we can only be protected collectively. And we have to reckon with the likelihood of circumstances in which these protections may be supplied only selectively and incompletely.

The Bill of Rights was written in anticipation both of the tendency of government to usurp the rights of individuals and of circumstances in which those rights will be hard to preserve. It would always be reasonable to foresee times of stress between the government's obligation to safeguard the lives of people and its obligation to respect their rights. This is the reason for appending a Bill of Rights to the Constitution.

However, the Bill of Rights insists that the rights of individual persons must be unfailingly respected in all circumstances excepting only one, which is set forth in Article V: "No person shall be held to answer for a capital, or otherwise infamous crime, unless on a presentment or indictment of a grand jury, except in cases arising in the land or naval forces, or in the militia, when in actual service in time of war or public danger . . ." This exception is made, apparently, to validate military courts. But Article V expressly disdains to limit its application merely to citizens; it says "No person," not "No citizen." And having stated the exception, it returns promptly to the inclusive language it began with: "nor shall any person ... be deprived of life, liberty, or property, without due process of law ..."

It is clear, then, that secret imprisonment by the government of *any person*, citizen or immigrant or alien or enemy, is necessarily a denial of due process of law, insofar as no person can at the same time be secretly imprisoned and publicly tried. (We now have only the government's word that the number of prisoners is, or was, seven hundred.)

A further point is somewhat harder to state, but I think it is no less obvious. Terrorism, against which the government without formally declaring war says we are "at war," at the same time that it seeks to circumvent the legal conventions of war, has certainly precipitated a time of public danger. How badly frightened the general public may be by this state of affairs is a question hard to answer. But the federal government and the courts have given evidence that they, as the terrorists intended, are badly frightened. They are so badly frightened as to believe that they have no choice but to sacrifice the rights of persons in deference to the government's need for secrecy. But it is an error to believe that these two "fundamental values" can somehow be justly "balanced" by the government or the courts, or that the people can judge responsibly between their rights, which they can easily know, and a proclaimed "need," which the government so far forbids them to know. The Constitution, anyhow, does not provide for its own suspension by the fearful in a time of war and public danger.

(2004)

Contempt for Small Places

NEWSPAPER EDITORIALS deplore such human-caused degradations of the oceans as the Gulf of Mexico's "dead zone," and reporters describe practices like "mountain removal" mining in eastern Kentucky. Some day we may finally understand the connections.

The health of the oceans depends on the health of rivers; the health of rivers depends on the health of small streams; the health of small streams depends on the health of their watersheds. The health of the water is exactly the same as the health of the land; the health of small places is exactly the same as the health of large places. As we know, disease is hard to confine. Because natural law is in force everywhere, infections move.

We cannot immunize the continents and the oceans against our contempt for small places and small streams. Small destructions add up, and finally they are understood collectively as large destructions. Excessive nutrient runoff from farms and animal factories in the Mississippi watershed has caused, in the Gulf of Mexico, a hypoxic or "dead zone" of five or six thousand square miles. In forty-odd years, strip mining in the Appalachian coal fields, culminating in mountain removal, has gone far toward the destruction of a whole region, with untold damage to the region's people, to watersheds, and to the waters downstream.

There is not a more exemplary history of our contempt for small places than that of Eastern Kentucky coal mining, which has enriched many absentee corporate shareholders and left the region impoverished and defaced. Coal industry representatives are now defending mountain removal—and its attendant damage to forests, streams, wells, dwellings, roads, and community life—by saying that in "10, 15, 20 years" the land will be restored, and that such mining has "created the [level] land" needed for further industrial development.

But when you remove a mountain you also remove the topsoil and the forest, and you do immeasurable violence to the ecosystem and the watershed. These things are not to be restored in ten or twenty years, or in ten or twenty hundred years. As for the manufacture of level places for industrial development, the supply has already far exceeded any foreseeable demand. And the devastation continues.

The contradictions in the state's effort "to balance the competing interests" were stated as follows by Ewell Balltrip, director of the Kentucky Appalachian Commission: "If you don't have mining, you don't have an economy, and if you don't have an economy you don't have a way for the people to live. But if you don't have environmental quality, you won't create the kind of place where people want to live."

Yes. And if the clearly foreseeable result is a region of flat industrial sites where nobody wants to live, we need a better economy.

(2004)

Rugged Individualism

THE CAREER OF RUGGED INDIVIDUALISM in America has run mostly to absurdity, tragic or comic. But it also has done us a certain amount of good. There was a streak of it in Thoreau, who went alone to jail in protest against the Mexican War. And that streak has continued in his successors who have suffered penalties for civil disobedience because of their perception that the law and the government were not always or necessarily right. This is individualism of a kind rugged enough, and it has been authenticated typically by its identification with a communal good.

The tragic version of rugged individualism is in the presumptive "right" of individuals to do as they please, as if there were no God, no legitimate government, no community, no neighbors, and no posterity. This is most frequently understood as the right to do whatever one pleases with one's property. One's property, according to this formulation, is one's own absolutely.

Rugged individualism of this kind has cost us dearly in lost topsoil, in destroyed forests, in the increasing toxicity of the world, and in annihilated species. When property rights become absolute they are invariably destructive, for then they are used to justify not only the abuse of things of permanent value for the temporary benefit of legal owners, but also the appropriation and abuse of things to which the would-be owners have no rights at all, but which can belong only to the public or to the entire community of living creatures: the atmosphere, the water cycle, wilderness, ecosystems, the possibility of life.

This is made worse when great corporations are granted the status of "persons," who then can also become rugged individuals, insisting on their right to do whatever they please with their property. Because of the over-whelming wealth and influence of these "persons," the elected representa-tives and defenders of "the people of the United States" become instead the representatives and defenders of the corporations.

It has become ever more clear that this sort of individualism has never proposed or implied any protection of the rights of all individuals, but instead has promoted a ferocious scramble in which more and more of the rights of "the people" have been gathered into the ownership of fewer and fewer of the greediest and most powerful "persons."

I have described so far what most of us would identify as the rugged in-dividualism of the political right. Now let us have a look at the left. The rugged individualism of the left believes that an individual's body is a pro-perty belonging to that individual absolutely: The owners of bodies may, by right, use them as they please, as if there were no God, no legitimate gov-ernment, no community, no neighbors, and no posterity. This supposed right is manifested in the democratizing of "sexual liberation"; in the pop-ular assumption that marriage has been "privatized" and so made subor-dinate to the wishes of individuals; in the proposition that the individual is "autonomous"; in the legitimation of abortion as birth control—in the denial, that is to say, that the community, the family, one's spouse, or even one's own soul might exercise a legitimate proprietary interest in the use one makes of one's body. And this too is tragic, for it sets us "free" from responsibility and thus from the possibility of meaning. It makes unintel-ligible the self-sacrifice that sent Thoreau to jail.

The comedy begins when these two rugged (or "autonomous") individ-ualisms confront each other. Conservative individualism strongly sup-ports "family values" and abominates lust. But it does not dissociate itself from the profits accruing from the exercise of lust (and, in fact, of the other six deadly sins), which it encourages in its advertisements. The "conserva-tives" of our day understand pride, lust, envy, anger, covetousness, glut-tony, and sloth as virtues when they lead to profit or to political power. Only as unprofitable or unauthorized personal indulgences do they rank as sins, imperiling salvation of the soul, family values, and national security.

Liberal individualism, on the contrary, understands sin as a private matter. It strongly supports protecting "the environment," which is that part of the world which surrounds, at a safe distance, the privately-owned body. "The environment" does not include the economic landscapes of agriculture and forestry or their human communities, and it does not include the privately-owned bodies of other people—all of which appear to have been bequeathed in fee simple to the corporate individualists.

Conservative rugged individualists and liberal rugged individualists believe alike that they should be "free" to get as much as they can of whatever they want. Their major doctrinal difference is that they want (some of the time) different sorts of things.

"Every man for himself" is a doctrine for a feeding frenzy or for a panic in a burning nightclub, appropriate for sharks or hogs or perhaps a cascade of lemmings. A society wishing to endure must speak the language of caretaking, faith-keeping, kindness, neighborliness, and peace. That language is another precious resource that cannot be "privatized."

(2004)

We Have Begun

THE TOPOGRAPHY of my native region of Kentucky was shaped by flowing water. The uplands are gently-rounded ridges divided by the valleys of streams that gather the runoff into the Kentucky River. There is some relatively flat land along the larger streams and the river. The valley sides are steep and now generally are forested. This is a broken, small-featured, mostly sloping landscape that erodes easily when the soil is exposed by cultivation.

To any knowledgeable person familiar with this place, a number of things are obvious:

1. This is land that needs to be farmed with great care by people who know it well.
2. It needs perennial vegetation—trees or grass.
3. The steeper slopes should be permanently forested.
4. In any year, most of the land that is not forested should be in grass.
5. Any farming that is done here should make use of grazing animals.
6. The bottomlands, ridgetops, and gentler slopes can be planted in row crops, but they should not be continuously in cultivation. On most farms no more than 5 or 10 percent should be plowed in any year. The crops should be grown in small plots or in strips. No land should remain in cultivation for more than a year or two.
7. Even grazing should be done with close attention and care, and on an appropriate scale, in order to avoid both overgrazing and the heavy treading that will expose the soil to erosion.

This, then, is a landscape best suited to a kind of farming that is small in

scale and highly diversified. And this is the kind of farming that was practiced here until the rapid industrialization of American agriculture following World War II. The farms were mostly small, with an average size of
about one hundred acres. Nearly all farms were locally owned. Most were
lived on and farmed by their owners.

Though every one of those farms produced for the market, they were
supported also by extensive household or subsistence economies. The
farms typically kept horses or mules for work, hogs and dairy cows for both
family and commercial use, and beef cattle or sheep or both. This region
was noted for the production of spring lambs. Every farm had a flock of
chickens, and often of other poultry. Every farm had a vegetable garden.
The major cash crop was tobacco, grown in small acreages, but every farm
also grew corn, and the small grains were sown in the fall on the tobacco
and corn fields, to be harvested the next summer. The grain crops were
more often fed than sold.

Such farming was traditional here. It was not uniformly good, and it had
not solved all its problems, but it was in many ways admirable. It could have
been built upon and improved.

We did not build upon it and improve it. Instead, we have allowed it to
be nearly destroyed by the methods and the economy of industrialism.
Now the farms are much larger and many fewer. Probably fewer than half
are lived on and farmed by their owners. The draft horses and mules, the
hogs and the sheep flocks, are nearly all gone. The local tobacco economy
has been nearly destroyed by globalization. The old subsistence economy
is virtually extinct.

Clearly, it is time for us to think again, and we are doing so. There is a
growing interest here in farmers markets, community supported agriculture, and other means of direct marketing to local customers, in diversifica-
tion, sustainable agriculture, Slow Food, and so forth. A lively, well-informed
conversation about agriculture is now well-established and going on.

It is always clearer, I believe, that the survival of farming in this region,
as in many others, cannot be secured by "competing on the global market."
To survive, our farmers are going to need a fully developed local land-based

economy supported by informed and locally-committed urban con-sumers. To achieve this will require a long time and a lot of work, but we have begun.

(2004)

Some Notes for the Kerry Campaign, If Wanted

FACING THIS YEAR'S PRESIDENTIAL election, our people are bitterly divided. This division is perhaps as great a threat to our future as is the possibility of a second term for Mr. Bush. And so the paramount question for Senator Kerry's campaign is how to oppose Mr. Bush effectively without so exacerbating the country's political differences as to reduce the possibility of effective government should Senator Kerry win the election.

One answer, I believe, is to base the campaign solidly and clearly upon our traditional principles of politics and religion. (I am reluctant to say that religion ought to be a political issue in the United States, but it is unstoppably an issue in this campaign.) If the campaign is based soundly enough on principles, then it can be carried out, at least by the Democrats, as a reasoned argument against the other side, and thus without sensationalizing personal and emotional differences. The further great advantage is that the Bush administration can be shown all too handily to be in violation of many of our country's traditional political and religious principles.

Our government was understood by its founders, and it is understood by many of us still, as a government of laws—of laws based in part on the laws of God. But the Bush administration, by various arrogations of power, has led us dangerously in the direction of autocracy. A government of laws cannot pardonably ignore either the rights of its citizens or its international treaties. A lot of people now long for national officials who are constantly and strictly mindful of our Bill of Rights.

Our government has a long—though imperfect and incomplete—

history of international cooperation, the good results of which are now seriously threatened by Mr. Bush's unilateralism and his doctrine of preemptive war.

Both our political and religious traditions instruct us that the truth makes us free. Our kind of government can govern effectively only by telling the truth, just as effective citizenship depends upon knowing the truth. Official secrecy and official lies, even in a good cause, carry us toward tyranny. Our government is meant to conduct the public's business in public.

Traditionally we have believed, and sometimes have acted on our belief, that political democracy depends upon a significant measure of economic democracy. Since World War II we have changed rapidly from a country owned by many people to a country owned by a few. This has been explicitly the program of some administrations, including that of Mr. Bush. We need an administration that is opposed to such a program. This country should not be entirely owned and run by the great corporations.

Our federal system was conceived as a way to balance national unity with local self-determination and self-sufficiency. Terrorism has now made local economic integrity more necessary than ever before. All the regions of our country are dangerously dependent on long-distance transportation. The emphasis in agriculture should now be on genetic diversity, local adaptation, and conservation of energy. We need, for a change, an agriculture policy to focus above all on the health of the land and the economic prosperity of the smaller farmers rather than on the enrichment of the agribusiness corporations.

Along with all the rest of the world's people, we have inherited ancient instructions for the stewardship and good husbandry of the earth, with clear warnings, now scientifically verified, of the disasters that will (and already do) attend our failure. We have responded by continuing our elaborately rationalized destructions. But bad precedent is no excuse for bad behavior. The Bush attitude toward the natural (the God-given) world is sacrilegious and wildly uneconomic.

The human norm, as established by Christ (and others), is love even for enemies, forgiveness, neighborliness, and peace. It is therefore troubling that members of the present administration, while making much of their commitment to Christ, are insisting on the normality of hatred, greed, revenge, and unremitting war. To make us afraid they speak much of the willingness of our terrorist enemies to kill themselves in order to kill us, as if this were an innovation. They forget, or they would like us to forget, that our policy of nuclear defense has been suicidal from the beginning. Our increasing destructiveness of the natural world is likewise suicidal. Such desperate security and prosperity cannot be reconciled with reverence for our Creator who endowed all humans with certain inalienable rights, including life.

However obscured by a history that has fallen short, our religious principles are justice, mercy, peaceableness, and loving-kindness toward fellow humans and the gifts of nature, as our political principles are freedom confirmed in law, honesty, and public accountability. These are not the principles of a party. They are our free inheritance as human beings and as citizens living under the Constitution of the United States.

(2004)

Compromise, Hell!*

WE ARE DESTROYING OUR COUNTRY—I mean our country itself, our land. This is a terrible thing to know, but it is not a reason for despair unless we decide to continue the destruction. If we decide to continue the destruction, that will not be because we have no other choice. This destruction is not necessary. It is not inevitable, except that by our submissiveness we make it so.

We Americans are not usually thought to be a submissive people, but of course we are. Why else would we allow our country to be destroyed? Why else would we be rewarding its destroyers? Why else would we all—by proxies we have given to greedy corporations and corrupt politicians—be participating in its destruction? Most of us are still too sane to piss in our own cistern, but we allow others to do so, and we reward them for it. We reward them so well, in fact, that those who piss in our cistern are wealthier than the rest of us.

How do we submit? By not being radical enough. Or by not being thorough enough, which is the same thing.

Since the beginning of the conservation effort in our country, conservationists have too often believed that we could protect the land without protecting the people. This has begun to change, but for a while yet we will have to reckon with the old assumption that we can preserve the natural world by protecting wilderness areas while we neglect or destroy the economic landscapes—the farms and ranches and working forests—and the people who use them. That assumption is understandable in view of the

*Written originally as a speech for the annual Earth Day celebration of the Kentucky Environmental Quality Commission at Frankfort, Kentucky, April 22, 2004.

worsening threats to wilderness areas, but it is wrong. If conservationists hope to save even the wild lands and wild creatures, they are going to have to address issues of economy, which is to say issues of the health of the land-scapes and the towns and cities where we do our work, and the quality of that work, and the well-being of the people who do the work.

Governments seem to be making the opposite error, believing that the people can be adequately protected without protecting the land. And here I am not talking about parties or party doctrines, but about the dominant political assumption. Sooner or later, governments will have to recognize that if the land does not prosper, nothing else can prosper for very long. We can have no industry or trade or wealth or security if we don't uphold the health of the land and the people and the people's work.

It is merely a fact that the land, here and everywhere, is suffering. We have the "dead zone" in the Gulf of Mexico and undrinkable water to attest to the toxicity of our agriculture. We know that we are carelessly and waste-fully logging our forests. We know that soil erosion, air and water pollu-tion, urban sprawl, the proliferation of highways and garbage are making our lives always less pleasant, less healthful, less sustainable, and our dwelling places more ugly.

Nearly forty years ago my state of Kentucky, like other coal-producing states, began an effort to regulate strip mining. While that effort has con-tinued, and has imposed certain requirements of "reclamation," strip mining has become steadily more destructive of the land and the land's future. We are now permitting the destruction of entire mountains and entire watersheds. No war, so far, has done such extensive or such perma-nent damage. If we know that coal is an exhaustible resource, whereas the forests over it are with proper use inexhaustible, and that strip mining destroys the forest virtually forever, how can we permit this destruction? If we honor at all that fragile creature the topsoil, so long in the making, so miraculously made, so indispensable to all life, how can we destroy it? If we believe, as so many of us profess to do, that the Earth is God's property and is full of His glory, how can we do harm to any part of it?

In Kentucky, as in other unfortunate states, and again at great public

cost, we have allowed—in fact we have officially encouraged—the estab-
lishment of the confined animal-feeding industry, which exploits and
abuses everything involved: the land, its people, the animals, and the consumers. If we love our country, as so many of us profess to do, how can we
so desecrate it?

But the economic damage is not confined just to our farms and forests.
For the sake of "job creation" in Kentucky, and in other backward states,
we have lavished public money on corporations that come in and stay
only so long as they can exploit people here more cheaply than elsewhere.
The general purpose of the present economy is to exploit, not to foster or
conserve.

Look carefully, if you doubt me, at the centers of the larger towns in virtually every part of our country. You will find that they are economically
dead or dying. Good buildings that used to house needful, useful, locally
owned small businesses of all kinds are now empty or have evolved into
junk stores or antique shops. But look at the houses, the churches, the commercial buildings, the courthouse, and you will see that more often than
not they are comely and well made. And then go look at the corporate outskirts: the chain stores, the fast-food joints, the food-and-fuel stores that
no longer can be called service stations, the motels. Try to find something
comely or well made there.

What is the difference? The difference is that the old town centers were
built by people who were proud of their place and who realized a particular value in living there. The old buildings look good because they were
built by people who respected themselves and wanted the respect of their
neighbors. The corporate outskirts, on the contrary, were built by people
who manifestly take no pride in the place, see no value in lives lived there,
and recognize no neighbors. The only value they see in the place is the
money that can be siphoned out of it to more fortunate places—that is, to
the wealthier suburbs of the larger cities.

Can we actually suppose that we are wasting, polluting, and making ugly
this beautiful land for the sake of patriotism and the love of God? Perhaps
some of us would like to think so, but in fact this destruction is taking place

because we have allowed ourselves to believe, and to live, a mated pair of economic lies: that nothing has a value that is not assigned to it by the market, and that the economic life of our communities can safely be handed over to the great corporations.

We citizens have a large responsibility for our delusion and our destructiveness, and I don't want to minimize that. But I don't want to minimize, either, the large responsibility that is borne by government.

It is commonly understood that governments are instituted to provide certain protections that citizens individually cannot provide for themselves. But governments have tended to assume that this responsibility can be fulfilled mainly by the police and the military services. They have used their regulatory powers reluctantly and often poorly. Our governments have only occasionally recognized the need of land and people to be protected against economic violence. It is true that economic violence is not always as swift, and is rarely as bloody, as the violence of war, but it can be devastating nonetheless. Acts of economic aggression can destroy a landscape or a community or the center of a town or city, and they routinely do so.

Such damage is justified by its corporate perpetrators and their political abettors in the name of the "free market" and "free enterprise," but this is a freedom that makes greed the dominant economic virtue, and it destroys the freedom of other people along with their communities and livelihoods. There are such things as economic weapons of massive destruction. We have allowed them to be used against us, not just by public submission and regulatory malfeasance, but also by public subsidies, incentives, and sufferances impossible to justify.

We have failed to acknowledge this threat and to act in our own defense. As a result, our once-beautiful and bountiful countryside has long been a colony of the coal, timber, and agribusiness corporations, yielding an immense wealth of energy and raw materials at an immense cost to our land and our land's people. Because of that failure also, our towns and cities have been gutted by the likes of Wal-Mart, which have had the permitted luxury of destroying locally owned small businesses by means of volume discounts.

Because as individuals or even as communities we cannot protect ourselves against these aggressions, we need our state and national governments to protect us. As the poor deserve as much justice from our courts as the rich, so the small farmer and the small merchant deserve the same economic justice, the same freedom in the market, as big farmers and chain stores. They should not suffer ruin merely because their rich competitors can afford (for a while) to undersell them.

Furthermore, to permit the smaller enterprises always to be ruined by false advantages, either at home or in the global economy, is ultimately to destroy local, regional, and even national capabilities of producing vital supplies such as food and textiles. It is impossible to understand, let alone justify, a government's willingness to allow the human sources of necessary goods to be destroyed by the "freedom" of this corporate anarchy. It is equally impossible to understand how a government can permit, and even subsidize, the destruction of the land or of the land's productivity. Somehow we have lost or discarded any controlling sense of the interdependence of the Earth and the human capacity to use it well. The governmental obligation to protect these economic resources, inseparably human and natural, is the same as the obligation to protect us from hunger or from foreign invaders. In result, there is no difference between a domestic threat to the sources of our life and a foreign one.

It appears that we have fallen into the habit of compromising on issues that should not, and in fact cannot, be compromised. I have an idea that a large number of us, including even a large number of politicians, believe that it is wrong to destroy the Earth. But we have powerful political opponents who insist that an Earth-destroying economy is justified by freedom and profit. And so we compromise by agreeing to permit the destruction only of parts of the Earth, or to permit the Earth to be destroyed a little at a time—like the famous three-legged pig that was too well loved to be eaten all at once.

The logic of this sort of compromising is clear, and it is clearly fatal. If we continue to be economically dependent on destroying parts of the Earth, then eventually we will destroy it all.

So long a complaint accumulates a debt to hope, and I would like to end with hope. To do so I need only repeat something I said at the beginning: Our destructiveness has not been, and it is not, inevitable. People who use that excuse are morally incompetent, they are cowardly, and they are lazy. Humans don't have to live by destroying the sources of their life. People can change; they can learn to do better. All of us, regardless of party, can be moved by love of our land to rise above the greed and contempt of our land's exploiters. This of course leads to practical problems, and I will offer a short list of practical suggestions.

We have got to learn better to respect ourselves and our dwelling places. We need to quit thinking of rural America as a colony. Too much of the economic history of our land has been that of the export of fuel, food, and raw materials that have been destructively and too cheaply produced. We must reaffirm the economic value of good stewardship and good work. For that we will need better accounting than we have had so far.

We need to reconsider the idea of solving our economic problems by "bringing in industry." Every state government appears to be scheming to lure in a large corporation from somewhere else by "tax incentives" and other squanderings of the people's money. We ought to suspend that practice until we are sure that in every state we have made the most and the best of what is already there. We need to build the local economies of our communities and regions by adding value to local products and marketing them locally before we seek markets elsewhere.

We need to confront honestly the issue of scale. Bigness has a charm and a drama that are seductive, especially to politicians and financiers; but bigness promotes greed, indifference, and damage, and often bigness is not necessary. You may need a large corporation to run an airline or to manufacture cars, but you don't need a large corporation to raise a chicken or a hog. You don't need a large corporation to process local food or local timber and market it locally.

And, finally, we need to give an absolute priority to caring well for our land—for every bit of it. There should be no compromise with the destruction of the land or of anything else that we cannot replace. We have been too tolerant of politicians who, entrusted with our country's defense, become the agents of our country's destroyers, compromising on its ruin.

And so I will end this by quoting my fellow Kentuckian, a great patriot and an indomitable foe of strip mining, the late Joe Begley of Blackey: "Compromise, hell!"

(2004)

Charlie Fisher

I DON'T IMAGINE Charlie Fisher told me everything he has done, but in the day and a half I spent with him I did find out that he was raised on a truck farm, that for a while he rode bulls and exhibited a trick horse on the rodeo circuit, that as a young man he worked for a dairyman, and that later he had a dairy farm of his own. His interest in logging and in working horses began while he was a hired hand in the dairy. In the winter, between milkings, he and his elderly employer spent their time in the woods at opposite ends of a crosscut saw—which, Charlie says, made him tireder than it made the old dairyman. They cut some big timber and dragged out the logs with horses. The old dairyman saw that Charlie liked working horses and was good at it. And so it was that he became both a teamster and a logger.

Though he tried other employment, those two early interests stayed with him, and he has spent many years in logging with horses. There were times when he worked alone, cutting and skidding out the logs by himself. Later, his son, David, began to work with him, skidding out the logs while Charlie cut. David, who is now twenty-two, virtually grew up in the woods. He started skidding logs with a team when he was nine, and he is still working with his father, as both teamster and log cutter.

Nine years ago, near Andover in northeast Ohio, Charlie Fisher and Jeff Green formed a company, Valley Veneer, which involves both a logging operation and a sawmill. Charlie buys the standing timber, marks the trees that are to be cut, and supervises the logging crews, while Jeff keeps things going at the mill and markets the lumber.

The mill employs eight or nine hands, and it saws three million board feet a year. It provides a local market for local timber. This obviously is good for the economy of the Andover neighborhood, but it also is good for the forest. By establishing the mill, Charlie and Jeff have invested in the neighborhood and formed a permanent connection to it, and so they have an inescapable interest in preserving the productivity of the local forest. Thus a local forest economy, if it is complex enough, will tend almost naturally to act as a conserver of the local forest ecosystem. Valley Veneer, according to Charlie and Jeff, has been warmly received into the neighborhood. The company deals with the only locally-owned bank in the area. The bankers have been not only cooperative but also friendly, at times offering more help than Charlie and Jeff asked for.

The mill yard is the neatest I have ever seen. The logs are sorted and ricked according to species. Veneer logs are laid down separately with one end resting on a pole, so that they can be readily examined by buyers. The mill crew is skillful in salvaging good lumber from damaged or inferior trees. This is extremely important, as is Jeff's marketing of lumber from inferior species such as soft maple, for it means that the cutting in the woods is never limited to the best trees. Charlie marks the trees, knowing that whatever the woodland can properly yield—soft maple or fine furniture-quality cherry or trees damaged by disease or wind—can be sawed into boards and sold. The mill seemed to me an extraordinarily efficient place, where nothing of value is wasted. Twenty percent of the slabs are sold for firewood; the rest go to the chipper and are used for pulp. The sawdust is sold to farmers, who use it as bedding for animals.

The woods operation—Charlie's end of the business—consists of three logging crews, each made up of one log cutter and two teamsters. Each of the teamsters works two horses on a logging cart or "logging arch." And so Charlie routinely employs nine men and twelve horses. At times, the cutter also will do some skidding, and this increases the number of teams in use. The three crews will usually be at work at three different sites.

Mostly they log small, privately-owned woodlots within a radius of forty or fifty miles. Charlie recently counted up and found that he had logged 366 different tracts of timber in the last three years. And there are certain advantages to working on this scale. In a horse logging operation, it is best to limit the skidding distance to five or six hundred feet, though Charlie says they sometimes increase it to a thousand, and they can go somewhat farther in winter when snow or freezing weather reduces the friction. Big tracts, however, involve longer distances, and eventually it becomes necessary either to build a road for the truck or to use a bulldozer to move the logs from where the teamsters yard them in the woods to a second yarding place accessible from the highway. For this purpose, in addition to a log truck equipped with a hydraulic loading boom, Valley Veneer owns two bulldozers, one equipped with a fork, one with a blade, and both with winches. Even so, about 98 percent of the logs are moved with horses.

The logging crews work the year round and in all weather except pouring rain. The teamsters, who furnish their own teams and equipment, receive forty dollars per thousand board feet. Two of his teamsters, Charlie says, make more than thirty thousand dollars a year each.

The logging arch, in comparison to a mechanical skidder, is a very forthright piece of equipment. Like the forecart that is widely used for fieldwork, it is simply a way to provide a drawbar for a team of horses. There are a number of differences in design, but the major one is that the logging arch's drawbar is welded on edge-up and has slots instead of holes. The slots are made so as to catch and hold the links of a log chain. Each cart carries an eighteen-foot chain with a grab hook at each end. Four metal hooks (which Charlie calls "log grabs," but which are also called "J-hooks" or "logging dogs") are linked to rings and strung on the chain, thus permitting the cart to draw as many as four logs at a time. The chain can also be used at full-length if necessary to reach a hard-to-get-to-log. Larger logs require the use of tongs, which the teamsters also carry with them, or two grabs driven into the log on opposite sides. The carts are equipped also with a cant hook and a "skipper" with which to drive the grabs into the log and knock them out again.

The slotted drawbar permits the chain to be handily readjusted as the horses work a log into position for skidding. When the log is ready to go, it is chained as closely as possible to the drawbar, so that when the horses tighten, the fore end of the log is raised off the ground. This is the major efficiency of the logging arch: By thus raising the log, the arch both keeps it from digging and reduces its friction against the ground by more than half.

We watched a team drag out a twelve-foot log containing about 330 board feet. They were well-loaded but were not straining. Charlie says that a team can handle up to five or six hundred board feet. For bigger logs, they use an additional team or a bulldozer. A good teamster can skid 3000 to 3500 board feet a day in small logs. The trick, Charlie says, is to know what your horses can do, and then see that they do that much on every pull. Overload, and you're resting too much. Underload, and you're wasting energy and time. The important thing is to keep loaded and keep moving.

Charlie Fisher is a man of long experience in the woods and extensive knowledge of the timber business and of logging technology. He has no prejudice against mechanical equipment as such, but uses it readily according to need; for a time, during his thirties, he used mechanical skidders. That this man greatly prefers horses for use in the woods is therefore of considerable interest. I asked him to explain.

His first reason, and the most important, is one I'd heard before from draft horsemen: "I've always liked horses." Charlie and David are clearly the sort of men who can't quite live without horses. Between them, they own six excellent, very large Belgian geldings and two Belgian mares. Charlie, as he explained, owns three and a half horses, and David four and a half. The two halves, fortunately, belong to the same horse, which Charlie and David own in partnership. Charlie has long been an enthusiastic participant in pulling contests, and David has followed in his father's footsteps in the arena as in the woods. Last season, David participated in twenty-three contests and Charlie in five, which for him was many fewer than usual. Charlie and his wife, Becky, showed us several shelves crowded with trophies, many of which were David's. It looked to me like they are going to need more shelves. Charlie and Becky are very proud of David, who is an accomplished logger and horseman. David, Charlie says, is an exceptionally quiet hand with a team—unlike Charlie, who confessed, "I holler." Since they would have the horses anyhow, Charlie said, they might as well put them to work in the woods, which keeps them fit and allows them to earn their keep.

Charlie's second reason for using horses in the woods, almost as important as the first, is that he likes the woods, and horses leave the woods in better condition than a skidder. A team and a logging arch require a much narrower roadway than a skidder; unlike a skidder, they don't bark trees; and they leave their skidding trails far less deeply rutted. "The horse," Charlie says, "will always be the answer to good logging in a woods."

A third attractive feature of the horse economy in the woods is that the horse logger both earns and spends his money in the local community, whereas the mechanical skidder siphons money away from the community and into the hands of large corporate suppliers. Moreover, the horse logger's kinder treatment of the woods will, in the long run, yield an economic benefit.

And, finally, horses work far more cheaply and cost far less than a skidder, thus requiring fewer trees to be cut per acre, and so permitting the horse logger to be more selective and conservative.

(Another issue involved in the use of horses for work is that of energy efficiency. Legs are more efficient than wheels over rough ground—something that will quickly be apparent to you if you try riding a bicycle over a plowed field.)

Well ahead of the logging crews, Charlie goes into the woods to mark the trees that are to be cut. Except when he is working for a "developer" who is going to clear the land, Charlie never buys or marks trees with the idea of taking every one that is marketable. His purpose is to select a number of trees, often those that need cutting because they are diseased or damaged or otherwise inferior, which will provide a reasonable income to landowner and logger alike, without destroying the wood-making capacity of the forest. The point can best be understood by considering the difference between a year's growth added to a tree fourteen inches in diameter and that added to a tree four inches in diameter. Clear-cutting or any other kind of cutting that removes all the trees of any appreciable size radically reduces the wood-making capacity of the forest. After such a cutting, in Charlie's part of the country, it will be sixty to a hundred years before another cutting can be made. Of a clear-cut woodland that adjoined one of his own tracts, Charlie said, "In fifty years there still won't be a decent log in it."

Charlie does not believe that such practices are good for the forest or the people—or, ultimately, for the timber business. He stated his interest forthrightly in economic terms, but his is the right kind of economics: "I hope maybe there'll be trees here for my son to cut in ten or twenty years." If you don't overdo the cutting, he says, a woodland can yield a cash crop every ten to fifteen years. We looked at one tract of twenty acres on which Charlie had marked about 160 trees and written the owner a check for $23,000. Charlie described this as "a young piece of timber," and he said that it "definitely" could be logged again in ten years—at which time he could both take more and leave more good trees than he will take and leave at this cutting.

Owners of wooded land should consider carefully the economics of this twenty-acre tract. If it is selectively and carefully logged every ten years, as Charlie says it can be, then every acre will earn $1,150 every ten years, or $115 per year. And this comes to the landowner without expense or effort. (These particular figures, of course, apply only to this particular woodlot. Some tracts might be more productive, others less.)

We looked at marked woodlands, at woodlands presently being logged, and finally, at the end of the second day of our visit, at a woodland that one of Charlie's crews had logged three years ago. The last, a stand predominantly of hard and soft maples, provided convincing evidence of the good sense of Charlie's kind of forestry. Very few of the remaining trees had been damaged by trees felled during the logging. I saw not a single tree that had been barked by a skidded log. The skid trails had completely healed over; there was no sign of erosion. And, most striking, the woodland was still ecologically intact. It was still a diverse, uneven-aged stand of trees, many of which were over sixteen inches in diameter. We made a photograph of three trees, standing fairly close together, which varied in diameter from seventeen to twenty-one inches. After logging, the forest is still a forest, and it will go on making wood virtually without interruption or diminishment. It seems perfectly reasonable to think that, if several generations of owners were so inclined, this sort of forestry could eventually result in an "old growth" forest that would have produced a steady income for two hundred years.

I was impressed by a good many things during my visit with Charlie Fisher, but what impressed me most is the way that Charlie's kind of logging achieves a complex fairness or justice to the several interests that are involved: the woods, the landowner, the timber company, the woods crews and their horses.

Charlie buys standing trees, and he marks every tree he buys. Within a fairly narrow margin of error, Charlie knows what he is buying, and the landowner knows what he is getting paid for. When Charlie goes in to mark the trees, he is thinking not just about what he will take, but also about what he will leave. He sees the forest as it is, and he sees the forest as it will be when the logging job is finished. I think he sees it too as it will be in ten or fifteen or twenty years, when David or another logger will return to it. By this long-term care, he serves the forest and the landowner as well as himself. As he marks the trees he is thinking also of the logging crew that will soon be there. He marks each tree that is to be cut with a slash of red paint. Sometimes, where he has seen a leaning deadfall or a dead limb or a flaw in the trunk, he paints an arrow above the slash, and this means "Look up!" The horses, like the men, are carefully borne in mind. Everywhere, the aim is to do the work in the best and the safest way.

Moreover, these are not competing interests, but seem rather to merge into one another. Thus one of Charlie's economic standards—"I hope maybe there'll be trees here for my son to cut in ten or twenty years"— becomes, in application, an ecological standard. And the ecological standard becomes, again, an economic standard as it proves to be good for business.

Most landowners, Charlie says, care how their woodlands are logged. Though they may need the income from their trees, they don't want to sacrifice the health or beauty of their woods in order to get it. Charlie's way of logging recommends itself to such people; he does not need to advertise.

As we were driving away from his house on the morning of our second day, one of the neighbors waved us to a stop. This man makes his living selling firewood, and he had learned of two people who wanted their woodlands logged by a horse logger. That is the way business comes to him, Charlie said. Like other horse loggers, he has all the work he can do, and more. It has been ten years since he has had to hunt for woodlots to log. He said, "Everybody else has buyers out running the roads, looking for timber." But he can't buy all that he is offered.

I don't know that I have ever met a man with more enthusiasms than Charlie Fisher. I have mentioned already his abounding interest in his family, in forestry, and in working and pulling horses, but I have neglected to say that he is also a coon hunter. This seems to me a most revealing detail. Here is a man who makes his living by walking the woods all day, and who then entertains himself by walking the woods at night.

He told me that he had a list of several things he had planned to do when he retired, but that now, at sixty-six, he is busier than ever.

"Well," I said, "you seem to be enjoying it."

"Oh," he said, "I *love* it!"

(1996)

Part II

Imagination in Place

BY AN INTERWORKING of chance and choice, I have happened to live nearly all my life in a place I don't remember not knowing. Most of my forebears for the last two hundred years could have said the same thing. I was born to people who knew this place intimately, and I grew up knowing it intimately. For a long time the intimacy was not very conscious, but I certainly did not grow up here thinking of the place as "subject matter," and I have never thought of it in that way. I have not lived here, or worked with my neighbors and my family, or listened to the storytellers and the rememberers, in order to be a writer. The place is precedent to my work, especially my fiction, and is, as I shall try to show, inevitably different from it.

By the same interworking of chance and choice, though somewhat expectably, I have lived here as a farmer. Except for one great-grandfather, all of my family that I know about have been farming people, and I grew up under instruction, principally from my father but also from others, to learn farming, to know the difference between good farming and bad, to regard the land as of ultimate value, and to admire and respect those who farmed well. I never heard a farmer spoken of as "just a farmer" or a farm woman as "just a housewife." To my father and his father especially, the knowledge of land and of farming was paramount. They thought the difference between a good farmer and a bad one was just as critical as the difference between a good politician and a bad one.

In 1964, after several years of wandering about, my wife, Tanya, and I returned to Kentucky with our two children and bought the property known as Lanes Landing, on the Kentucky River, about a mile from the house where my mother was born and raised and about five miles from my father's home place. The next summer we fixed up the house and moved in. We have been here ever since, and our children are farming nearby.

Before we moved here, I had known this place for thirty-one years, and we have now lived here for thirty-nine. We raised our children here. We have taken from this place most of our food, much of our fuel, and always, despite the difficulties and frustrations of a farming life, a sustaining pleasure. Also, nearly everything I have written has been written here. When I am asked how all this fits together, I have to say, "Awkwardly."

This essay is most immediately obstructed by the difficulty of separating my work from my life, and the place from either. The place included in my work is also the place that has included me as a farmer and as a writer.

In the course of my life and of my work as a farmer, I have come to know familiarly two small country towns and about a dozen farms. That is, I have come to know them well enough at one time or another that I can shut my eyes and see them as they were, just as I can see them now as they are. The most intimate "world" of my life is thus a small one. The most intimate "world" of my fiction is even smaller: a town of about a hundred people, "Port William," and a few farms in its neighborhood. Between these two worlds, the experienced and the imagined, there is certainly a relationship. But it is a relationship obscure enough as it is, and easy to obscure further by oversimplification.

As a lot of writers must know, it is easy for one's family or neighbors to identify fictional characters with actual people. A lot of writers must know too that these identifications are sometimes astonishingly wrong, and are always at least a little wrong. The inevitability of this sort of error is explainable, and it is significant.

Some of my own fiction has seemed to me to be almost entirely imagined. Some of it has drawn maybe as close as possible to actual experience. The writing has sometimes grown out of a long effort to come to terms with an actual experience. But one must not be misled by the claims of "realism." There is, true enough, a kind of writing that has an obligation to tell the truth about actual experience, and therefore it is obliged to accept the limits of what is actually or provably known. But insofar as writing is a work of imagination, it comes of an impulse to transcend the limits of experience or provable knowledge in order to make a thing that is whole. Of course no human work can become whole by including everything, but it can become whole in another way: by accepting its formal limits and then answering within those limits all the questions it raises. Any reasonably literate reader can understand Homer without the benefit of archaeology, or Shakespeare without resort to his literary sources.

It seems to me that my effort to come to terms in writing with an actual experience has been, every time, an effort to imagine the experience, to see it clear and whole in the mind's eye. One might suppose, reasonably enough, that this could be accomplished by describing accurately what one actually knows from records of some sort or from memory. But this, I believe, is wrong. What one actually or provably knows about an actual experience is never complete; it cannot, within the limits of memory or factual records, be made whole. Imagination "completes the picture" by transcending the actual memories and provable facts. For this reason, I have often begun with an actual experience and in the end produced what I have had to call a fiction. In the effort to tell a whole story, to see it whole and clear, I have had to imagine more than I have known. "There's no use in telling a pretty good story when you can tell a really good one," my mother's father told me once. In saying so, he acknowledged both a human limit and a human power, as well as his considerable amusement at both.

----------◆----------

I believe I can say properly that my fiction originates in part in actual experience of an actual place: its topography, weather, plants, and animals; its language, voices, and stories. The fiction I have written here, I suppose, must somehow belong here and must be different from any fiction I might have written in any other place. I am pleased to suppose so, but the influence of this place alone cannot account for the fiction and the other work I have written here.

Both my writing and my involvement with this place have been in every way affected by my reading. My work would not exist as it is if the influence of this place were somehow subtracted from it. Just as certainly it would not exist as it is, if at all, without my literary mentors, exemplars, teachers, and guides. Lists are dangerous, but as a placed writer I have depended on the examples of Andrew Marvell at Appleton House, Jane Austen in Hampshire, Thomas Hardy in Dorset, Mark Twain in Hannibal, Thoreau in Concord, Sarah Orne Jewett on the Maine coast, Yeats in the west of Ireland, Frost in New England, William Carlos Williams in Rutherford, William Faulkner and Eudora Welty in Mississippi, Wallace Stegner in the American West, and in Kentucky, James Still, Harlan Hubbard, and Harry Caudill—to name only some of the dead and no contemporaries. Over the years I have kept fairly constantly in my mind the Bible, Homer, Dante, Shakespeare, Herbert, Milton, and Blake. I have taken much consolation and encouragement from Paul Cézanne's devotion to his home landscapes in Provence and Samuel Palmer's work at Shoreham. I have remembered often the man of Psalm 128 who shall eat the labor of his hands, and of Virgil's (and Ronsard's) old Cilician of *Georgics IV*. Over the last twenty years or so, I have contracted a large debt to certain writers about religious and cultural tradition, principally Ananda Coomaraswamy, Titus Burckhardt, Kathleen Raine, and Philip Sherrard—again, to name only the dead. Now that I have listed these names, I am more aware than before how incomplete any such list necessarily must be.

I will allow the list to stand, not as an adequate explanation, but as a hint at the difficulty of locating the origins of a work of fiction by me (or, I assume, by anybody else). And I must add further to the difficulty by saying that I don't believe I am conscious of all the sources of my work. I dislike learned talk about "the unconscious," which always seems to imply that the very intelligent are able somehow to know what they don't know, but I mean only to acknowledge that much of what I have written has taken me by surprise. What I know does not yield a full or adequate accounting for what I have imagined. It seems to have been "given." My experience has taught me to believe in inspiration, about which I think nobody can speak with much authority.

--------◆--------

My fiction, anyhow, has come into being within the contexts of local geography and local culture, of the personal culture of reading, listening, and looking, and also within the contexts of what is not known and of the originating power we call inspiration. But there is another context, that of agriculture, which I will need to deal with at more length.

I was brought up, as I have said, by agrarians and was conscientiously instructed in a set of assumptions and values that could be described only as agrarian. But I never saw that word in print or heard it pronounced until I was a sophomore at the University of Kentucky. At that time I was in a composition class whose instructor, Robert D. Jacobs, asked us to write an argument. I wrote, as I recall, a dialogue between two farmers on the condemnation of land for the construction of a highway or an airport. The gist of my argument was that the land was worth more than anything for which it might be destroyed. Dr. Jacobs didn't think much of my argument, but he did me a valuable service by identifying it as "agrarian" and referring me to a group of writers, "the Southern Agrarians," who had written a book called *I'll Take My Stand*. I bought the book and read at least part of it about three years later, in 1956. It is a valuable book, in some ways a wonder, and I have returned to it many times since. My debt to it has increased.

I must have become a good deal interested in the Southern Agrarians during my last years at the university, for with my friend and fellow student Mac Coffman (Edward M. Coffman, the historian) I drove up to Kenyon College to talk with John Crowe Ransom on that subject. But it is hard now for me to tell how much I may have been influenced by the Southern Agrarians and their book at that time. Ransom by then was disaffected from *I'll Take My Stand* (though his elegant introduction, "A Statement of Principles," is still the best summary of agrarian principles versus the principles of industrialism). And I think I encountered not much at the University of Kentucky that would have confirmed my native agrarianism. It seems to me now that my agrarian upbringing and my deepest loyalties were obscured by my formal education. Only after I returned to Kentucky in 1964 did I begin to reclaim what I had been taught at home as a growing boy. Once I was home again, the purpose and point of that teaching became clear to me as it had not before, and I became purposefully and eagerly an agrarian. Moreover, because I had settled here as a farmer, I knew that I was not a literary agrarian merely but also a practical one.

In 1970 I published in the *Southern Review* a small essay, "The Regional Motive," that I suppose was descended from, or at least a cousin to, the essays of *I'll Take My Stand*. But in my essay I said that "the withdrawal of the most gifted of [the Southern Agrarians] into…Northern colleges and universities invalidated their thinking, and reduced their effort to the level of an academic exercise." Whatever the amount of truth in that statement, and there is some, it is also a piece of smartassery.

I received in response a letter from Allen Tate. As I knew, Tate could be a combative man, and so I was moved, as I still am, by the kindness of his letter. He simply pointed out to me that I did not know the pressing reasons why he and his friends had moved to the North. And so when I reprinted my essay I added a footnote apologizing for my callowness and ignorance, but saying even so, and as I remember with Tate's approval, that I might appropriately "warn that their departure should not be taken either as disproof of the validity of their [agrarian] principles, or as justification of absentee regionalism (agrarianism without agriculture)."

The parentheses around that concluding phrase suggest to me now that I was making a point I had not quite got. The phrase, which appears to have been only an afterthought thirty-two years ago, points to what now seems to me the major fault of *I'll Take My Stand*: The agrarianism of most of the essays, like the regionalism of most of them, is abstract, too purely mental. The book is not impractical—none of its principles, I believe, is in conflict with practicality—but it is too often remote from the issues of practice. The legitimate aim (because it is the professed aim) of agrarianism is not some version of culture but good farming, though a culture complete enough may be implied in that aim. By 1970 I had begun to see the flaws and dangers of absentee regionalism, and especially of southern absentee regionalism. Identifying with "The South," as if it were somehow all one and the same place, would not help you to write any more than it would help you to farm. As a regional book, *I'll Take My Stand* mostly ignores the difficulty and the discipline of locality. As an agrarian book, it mostly ignores also the difficulty and the discipline of farming, but this problem is more complicated, and dealing with it took me longer.

Of the twelve essayists, only Andrew Lytle and John Donald Wade appear to speak directly from actual knowledge of actual farming in an actual place. And a passage of Andrew Lytle's essay, "The Hind Tit," points the direction I now must take with this essay of mine. He has begun to write about "a type" of farmer who has two hundred acres of land, but he does so with a necessary precaution:

> This example is taken, of course, with the knowledge that the problem on any two hundred acres is never the same: the richness of the soil, its qualities, the neighborhood, the distance from market, the climate, water, and a thousand such things make the life on every farm distinctly individual.

Thus he sets forth the fundamental challenge, not only to all forms of industrial land use, but to all other approaches to land use, including agrarianism, that are abstract.

The most insistent and formidable concern of agriculture, wherever it is taken seriously, is the distinct individuality of every farm, every field on every farm, every farm family, and every creature on every farm. Farming becomes a high art when farmers know and respect in their work the distinct individuality of their place and the neighborhood of creatures that lives there. This has nothing to do with the set of personal excuses we call "individualism" but is akin to the holy charity of the Gospels and the political courtesy of the Declaration of Independence and the Bill of Rights. Such practical respect is the true discipline of farming, and the farmer must maintain it through the muddles, mistakes, disappointments, and frustrations, as well as the satisfactions and exultations, of every actual year on an actual farm.

--------◆--------

And so it has mattered, undoubtedly it has mattered to my fiction, that I have lived in this place both as a farmer and as a writer. I am not going to pretend here to a judgment or criticism of the writing I have done. I mean only to say something about the pressures and conditions that have been imposed on my writing by my life here as a farmer. Rather than attempt to say what I have done, I will attempt to speak of farming as an influence.

Having settled even in so marginal a place as this, undertaking to live in it even by such marginal farming as I have done, one is abruptly and forcibly removed from easy access to the abstractions of regionalism, politics, economics, and the academic life. To farm is to be placed absolutely. To do the actual work of an actual farm one must shed the clichés that constitute "The South" or "My Old Kentucky Home" and come to the ground.

One may begin as an agrarian, as some of us to our good fortune have done, but for a farmer agrarianism is not enough. Southern agrarianism is not enough, and neither is Kentucky agrarianism or Henry County agrarianism. None of those can be local enough or particular enough. To live as a farmer, one has to come into the local watershed and the local ecosystem and deal well or poorly with them. One must encounter directly and feelingly the topography and the soils of one's particular farm, and treat them well or poorly.

If one wishes to farm well, and agrarianism inclines to that wish above all, then one must submit to the unending effort to change one's mind and ways to fit one's farm. This is a hard education, which lasts all one's life, never to be completed, and it almost certainly will involve mistakes. But one does not have to do this alone, or only with one's own small intelligence. Help is available, as one had better hope.

In my farming I have relied most directly on my family and my neighbors, who have helped me much and taught me much. And my thoughts about farming have been founded on a few wonderful books: *Farmers of Forty Centuries* by F. H. King, *An Agricultural Testament* and *The Soil and Health* by Sir Albert Howard, *Tree Crops* by J. Russell Smith, and *A Sand County Almanac* by Aldo Leopold. These writers bring the human economy face to face with ecology, the local landscape, and the farm itself. They teach us to think of the ecological problems and obligations of agriculture, and they do this by seeing in nature the inescapable standard and in natural processes the necessary pattern for any human use of the land. Their thinking has had its finest scientific result thus far in the "Natural Systems Agriculture" of the Land Institute in Salina, Kansas. Natural Systems Agriculture returns to the classical conception of art as an imitation of nature. But whereas Hamlet saw art as holding a mirror up to nature, and thus in a sense taking its measure, these agricultural thinkers have developed as well the balancing concept of nature as the inevitable mirror and measure of art.

In addition to books specifically about agriculture and ecology, I have been steadily mindful, as a farmer, of the writers mentioned earlier as literary influences. And I have depended for many years on the writing and the conversation of my friends Gene Logsdon, Maurice Telleen, Wes Jackson, and David Kline. I have been helped immeasurably also by the examples of Amish agriculture, of the traditional farming of Tuscany as I saw it more than forty years ago, of the ancient agricultures of the Peruvian Andes and the deserts of the American Southwest, of the also ancient pastoral landscapes of Devonshire, and of the best farming here at home as I knew it in the 1940s and early 1950s before industrialization broke up the old pattern.

What I have learned as a farmer I have learned also as a writer, and vice versa. I have farmed as a writer and written as a farmer. This is an experience that is resistant to any kind of simplification. I will go ahead and call it complexification. When I am called, as to my astonishment I sometimes am, a devotee of "simplicity" (since I live supposedly as a "simple farmer"), I am obliged to reply that I gave up the simple life when I left New York City in 1964 and came here. In New York, I lived as a passive consumer, supplying nearly all my needs by purchase, whereas here I supply many of my needs from this place by my work (and pleasure) and am responsible besides for the care of the place.

My point is that when one passes from any abstract order, whether that of the consumer economy or Ransom's "Statement of Principles" or a brochure from the Extension Service, to the daily life and work of one's own farm, one passes from a relative simplicity into a complexity that is irreducible except by disaster and ultimately is incomprehensible. It is the complexity of the life of a place uncompromisingly itself, which is at the same time the life of the world, of all Creation. One meets not only the weather and the wildness of the world, but also the limitations of one's knowledge, intelligence, character, and bodily strength. To do this, of course, is to accept the place as an influence.

My further point is that to do this, if one is a writer, is to accept the place and the farming of it as a literary influence. One accepts the place, that is, not just as a circumstance, but as a part of the informing ambience of one's mind and imagination. I don't dare to claim that I know how this "works," but I have no doubt at all that it is true. And I don't mind attempting some speculations on what might be the results.

To begin with, the work of a farmer, or of the sort of farmer I have been, is particularizing work. As farmers themselves never tire of repeating, you can't learn to farm by reading a book. You can't lay out a fence line or shape a plowland or fell a tree or break a colt merely by observing general principles. You can't deal with things merely according to category; you are continually required to consider the distinct individuality of an animal or a tree, or the uniqueness of a place or a situation, and to do so you draw upon a long accumulation of experience, your own and other people's. Moreover, you are always under pressure to explain to somebody (often yourself) exactly what needs to be done. All this calls for an exactly particularizing language. This is the right kind of language for a writer, a language developing, so to speak, from the ground up. It is the right kind of language for anybody, but a lot of our public language now seems to develop downward from a purpose. Usually, the purpose is to mislead, the particulars being selected or invented to suit the purpose; or the particulars dangle loosely and unregarded from the dislocated intellectuality of the universities. This is contrary to honesty and also to practicality.

The ability to speak exactly is intimately related to the ability to know exactly. In any practical work such as farming, the penalties for error are sometimes promptly paid, and this is valuable instruction for a writer. A farmer who is a writer will at least call farming tools and creatures by their right names, will be right about the details of work, and may extend the same courtesy to other subjects.

A writer who is a farmer will in addition be apt actually to know some actual country people, and this is a significant advantage. Reading some fiction, and this applies especially to some southern fiction, one cannot avoid the impression that the writers don't know any country people and are afraid of them. They fill the blank, not with anybody they have imagined, but with the rhetorically conjured stereotype of the hick or hillbilly or redneck who is the utter opposite of the young woman with six arms in the picture by the late ("Alas") Emmeline Grangerford, and perhaps is her son. He comes slouching into the universe with his pistol in one hand, his prong in another, his Bible in another, his bottle in another, his grand-pappy's cavalry sword in another, his plug of chewing tobacco in another. This does harm. If you wish to steal farm products or coal or timber from a rural region, you will find it much less troubling to do so if you can believe that the people are too stupid and violent to deserve the things you wish to steal from them. And so purveyors of rural stereotypes have served a predatory economy. Two of the Southern Agrarians, I should add, countered this sort of thing with knowledge. I am thinking of John Donald Wade's essay "The Life and Death of Cousin Lucius" in *I'll Take My Stand*, and *A Wake for the Living* by Andrew Lytle.

If you understand that what you do as a farmer will be measured inescapably by its effect on the place, and of course on the place's neighborhood of humans and other creatures, then if you are also a writer, you will have to wonder too what will be the effect of your writing on that place.

Obviously this is going to be hard for anybody to know, and you yourself may not live long enough to know it, but in your own mind you are going to be using the health of the place as one of the indispensable standards of what you write, thus dissolving the university and "the literary world" as adequate contexts for literature. It also is going to skew your work away from the standard of realism. "How things really are" is one of your concerns, but by no means the only one. You have begun to ask also how things will be, how you want things to be, how things ought to be. You want to know what are the meanings, both temporal and eternal, of the condition of things in this world. "Realism," as Kathleen Raine said, "cannot show us what we are, but only our failure to become that to which the common man and the common woman inadequately, but continually, aspire and strive." If, in other words, you want to write a whole story about whole people—living souls, not "higher animals"—you must reach for a reality that is inaccessible merely to observation or perception but that also requires imagination, for imagination knows more than the eye sees, and inspiration, which you can only hope and pray for. You will find, I think, that this effort involves even a sort of advocacy. Advocacy, as a lot of people will affirm, is dangerous to art, and you must beware the danger, but if you accept the health of the place as a standard, I think the advocacy is going to be present in your work. Hovering over nearly everything I have written is the question of how a human economy might be conducted with reverence, and therefore with due respect and kindness toward everything involved. This, if it ever happens, will be the maturation of American culture.

----------◆----------

I have tried (clumsily, I see) to define the places, real and imagined, where I have taken my stand and done my work. I have made the imagined place of Port William, its neighborhood and membership, in an attempt to honor the actual place where I have lived. By means of the imagined place, over the last fifty years, I have learned to see my native landscape and neighborhood as a place unique in the world, a work of God, possessed of an inherent sanctity that mocks any human valuation that can be put upon it. If anything I have written in this place can be taken to countenance the misuse of it, or to excuse anybody for rating the land as "capital" or its human members as "labor," my writing would have been better unwritten. And then to hell with any value anybody may find in it "as literature."

(2004)

The Way of Ignorance*

In order to arrive at what you do not know
You must go by a way which is the way of ignorance.
T. S. Eliot, "East Coker"

OUR PURPOSE HERE is to worry about the predominance of the supposition, in a time of great technological power, that humans either know enough already, or can learn enough soon enough, to foresee and forestall any bad consequences of their use of that power. This supposition is typified by Richard Dawkins's assertion, in an open letter to the Prince of Wales, that "our brains...are big enough to see into the future and plot long-term consequences."

When we consider how often and how recently our most advanced experts have been wrong about the future, and how often the future has shown up sooner than expected with bad news about our past, Mr. Dawkins's assessment of our ability to know is revealed as a superstition of the most primitive sort. We recognize it also as our old friend hubris, ungodly ignorance disguised as godly arrogance. Ignorance plus arrogance plus greed sponsors "better living with chemistry," and produces the ozone hole and the dead zone in the Gulf of Mexico. A modern science (chemistry or nuclear physics or molecular biology) "applied" by ignorant arrogance resembles much too closely an automobile being driven by a six-year-old or a loaded pistol in the hands of a monkey. Arrogant ignorance promotes a global economy while ignoring the global exchange of pests

---

*Written as a preliminary paper for a conference of the same title at the Land Institute, Matfield Green, Kansas, June 3–5, 2004. The purpose of the conference is stated in my first paragraph.

and diseases that must inevitably accompany it. Arrogant ignorance makes war without a thought of peace.

We identify arrogant ignorance by its willingness to work on too big a scale, and thus to put too much at risk. It fails to foresee bad consequences not only because some of the consequences of all acts are inherently unforeseeable, but also because the arrogantly ignorant often are blinded by money invested; they cannot afford to foresee bad consequences.

Except to the arrogantly ignorant, ignorance is not a simple subject. It is perhaps as difficult for ignorance to be aware of itself as it is for awareness to be aware of itself. One can hardly begin to think about ignorance without seeing that it is available in several varieties, and so I will offer a brief taxonomy.

There is, to begin with, the kind of ignorance we may consider to be inherent. This is ignorance of all that we cannot know because of the kind of mind we have—which, I will note in passing, is neither a computer nor exclusively a brain, and which certainly is not omniscient. We cannot, for example, know the whole of which we and our minds are parts. The English poet and critic Kathleen Raine wrote that "we cannot imagine how the world might appear if we did not possess the groundwork of knowledge which we do possess; nor can we in the nature of things imagine how reality would appear in the light of knowledge which we do not possess."

A part of our inherent ignorance, and surely a most formidable encumbrance to those who presume to know the future, is our ignorance of the past. We know almost nothing of our history as it was actually lived. We know little of the lives even of our parents. We have forgotten almost everything that has happened to ourselves. The easy assumption that we have remembered the most important people and events and have preserved the most valuable evidence is immediately trumped by our inability to know what we have forgotten.

There are several other kinds of ignorance that are not inherent in our nature but come instead from weaknesses of character. Paramount among these is the willful ignorance that refuses to honor as knowledge anything not subject to empirical proof. We could just as well call it materialist ignorance. This ignorance rejects useful knowledge such as traditions of imagination and religion, and so it comes across as narrow-mindedness. We have the materialist culture that afflicts us now because a world exclusively material is the kind of world most readily used and abused by the kind of mind the materialists think they have. To this kind of mind, there is no longer a legitimate wonder. Wonder has been replaced by a research agenda, which is still a world away from demonstrating the impropriety of wonder. The materialist conservationists need to tell us how a materialist culture can justify its contempt and destructiveness of material goods.

A related kind of ignorance, also self-induced, is moral ignorance, the invariable excuse of which is objectivity. One of the purposes of objectivity, in practice, is to avoid coming to a moral conclusion. Objectivity, considered a mark of great learning and the highest enlightenment, loves to identify itself by such pronouncements as the following: "You may be right, but on the other hand so may your opponent," or "Everything is relative," or "Whatever is happening is inevitable," or "Let me be the devil's advocate." (The part of devil's advocate is surely one of the most sought after in all the precincts of the modern intellect. Anywhere you go to speak in defense of something worthwhile, you are apt to encounter a smiling savant writhing in the estrus of objectivity: "Let me play the devil's advocate for a moment." As if the devil's point of view will not otherwise be adequately represented.)

There is also ignorance as false confidence, or polymathic ignorance. This is the ignorance of people who know "all about" history or its "long-term consequences" in the future. And this is closely akin to self-righteous ignorance, which is the failure to know oneself. Ignorance of one's self and confident knowledge of the past and future often are the same thing.

Fearful ignorance is the opposite of confident ignorance. People keep themselves ignorant for fear of the strange or the different or the unknown, for fear of disproof or of unpleasant or tragic knowledge, for fear of stirring up suspicion and opposition, or for fear of fear itself. A good example is the United States Department of Agriculture's panic-stricken monopoly of inadequate meat inspections. And there is the related ignorance that comes from laziness, which is the fear of effort and difficulty. Learning often is not fun, and this is well-known to all the ignorant except for a few "educators."

And finally there are for-profit ignorance, which is maintained by withholding knowledge, as in advertising, and for-power ignorance, which is maintained by government secrecy and public lies.

Kinds of ignorance (and there must be more than I have named) may thus be sorted out. But having sorted them out, one must scramble them back together again by acknowledging that all of them can be at work in the same mind at the same time, and in my opinion they frequently are.

I may be talking too much at large here, but I am going to say that a list of kinds of ignorance comprises half a description of a human mind. The other half, then, would be supplied by a list of kinds of knowledge.

At the head of that list let us put the empirical or provable knowledge of the materialists. This is the knowledge of dead certainty or dead facts, some of which at least are undoubtedly valuable, undoubtedly useful, but at best this is static, smallish knowledge that always is what it always was, and it is rather dull. A fact may thrill us once, but not twice. Once available, it is easy game; we might call it sitting-duck knowledge. This knowledge becomes interesting again when it enters experience by way of use.

And so, as second, let us put knowledge as experience. This is useful knowledge, but it involves uncertainty and risk. How do you know if it is going to rain, or when an animal is going to bolt or attack? Because the event has not yet happened, there is no empirical answer; you may not have time to calculate the statistical probability even on the fastest computer. You will have to rely on experience, which will increase your chance of being right. But then you also may be wrong.

The experience of many people over a long time is traditional knowledge. This is the common knowledge of a culture, which it seems that few of us any longer have. To have a culture, mostly the same people have to live mostly in the same place for a long time. Traditional knowledge is knowledge that has been remembered or recorded, handed down, pondered, corrected, practiced, and refined over a long time.

A related kind of knowledge is made available by the religious traditions and is not otherwise available. If you premise the falsehood of such knowledge, as the materialists do, then of course you don't have it and your opinion of it is worthless.

There also are kinds of knowledge that seem to be more strictly inward. Instinct is inborn knowledge: how to suck, bite, and swallow; how to run away from danger instead of toward it. And perhaps the prepositions refer to knowledge that is more or less instinctive: up, down, in, out, etc.

Intuition is knowledge as recognition, a way of knowing without proof. We know the truth of the Book of Job by intuition.

What we call conscience is knowledge of the difference between right and wrong. Whether or not this is learned, most people have it, and they appear to get it early. Some of the worst malefactors and hypocrites have it in full; how else could they fake it so well? But we should remember that some worthy people have believed conscience to be innate, an "inner light."

Inspiration, I believe, is another kind of knowledge or way of knowing, though I don't know how this could be proved. One can say in support only that poets such as Homer, Dante, and Milton seriously believed in it, and that people do at times surpass themselves, performing better than all you know of them has led you to expect. Imagination, in the highest sense, is inspiration. Gifts arrive from sources that cannot be empirically located.

Sympathy gives us an intimate knowledge of other people and other creatures that can come in no other way. So does affection. The knowledge that comes by sympathy and affection is little noticed—the materialists, I assume, are unable to notice it—but in my opinion it cannot be overvalued.

Everybody who has done physical work or danced or played a game of skill is aware of the difference between knowing how and being able. This difference I would call bodily knowledge.

And finally, to be safe, we had better recognize that there is such a thing as counterfeit knowledge or plausible falsehood.

-------◆-------

I would say that these taxonomies of mine are more or less reasonable; I certainly would not claim that they are scientific. My only assured claim is that any consideration of ignorance and knowledge ought to be at least as complex as this attempt of mine. We are a complex species—organisms surely, but also living souls—who are involved in a life-or-death negotiation, even more complex, with our earthly circumstances, which are complex beyond our ability to guess, let alone know. In dealing with those circumstances, in trying "to see into the future and plot long-term consequences," the human mind is neither capacious enough nor exact nor dependable. We are encumbered by an inherent ignorance perhaps not significantly reducible, as well as by proclivities to ignorance of other kinds, and our ways of knowing, though impressive within human limits, have the power to lead us beyond our limits, beyond foresight and precaution, and out of control.

What I have said so far characterizes the personal minds of individual humans. But because of a certain kind of arrogant ignorance, and because of the gigantic scale of work permitted and even required by powerful technologies, we are not safe in dealing merely with personal or human minds. We are obliged to deal also with a kind of mind that I will call corporate, although it is also political and institutional. This is a mind that is compound and abstract, materialist, reductionist, greedy, and radically utilitarian. Assuming as some of us sometimes do that two heads are better than one, it ought to be axiomatic that the corporate mind is better than any personal mind, but it can in fact be much worse—not least in its apparently limitless ability to cause problems that it cannot solve, and that may be unsolvable. The corporate mind is remarkably narrow. It claims to utilize only empirical knowledge—the preferred term is "sound science," reducible ultimately to the "bottom line" of profit or power—and because this rules out any explicit recourse to experience or tradition or any kind of inward knowledge such as conscience, this mind is readily susceptible to every kind of ignorance and is perhaps naturally predisposed to counterfeit knowledge. It comes to its work equipped with factual knowledge and perhaps also with knowledge skillfully counterfeited, but without recourse to any of those knowledges that enable us to deal appropriately with mystery or with human limits. It has no humbling knowledge. The corporate mind is arrogantly ignorant by definition.

Ignorance, arrogance, narrowness of mind, incomplete knowledge, and counterfeit knowledge are of concern to us because they are dangerous; they cause destruction. When united with great power, they cause great destruction. They have caused far too much destruction already, too often of irreplaceable things. Now, reasonably enough, we are asking if it is possible, if it is even thinkable, that the destruction can be stopped. To some people's surprise, we are again backed up against the fact that knowledge is not in any simple way good. We have often been a destructive species, we are more destructive now than we have ever been, and this, in perfect accordance with ancient warnings, is because of our ignorant and arrogant use of knowledge.

Before going further, we had better ask what it is that we humans need to know. We need to know many things, of course, and many kinds of things. But let us be merely practical for the time being and say that we need to know who we are, where we are, and what we must do to live. These questions do not refer to discreet categories of knowledge. We are not likely to be able to answer one of them without answering the other two. And all three must be well answered before we can answer well a further practical question that is now pressing urgently upon us: How can we work without doing irreparable damage to the world and its creatures, including ourselves? Or: How can we live without destroying the sources of our life?

These questions are perfectly honorable, we may even say that they are perfectly obvious, and yet we have much cause to believe that the corporate mind never asks any of them. It does not care who it is, for it is not anybody; it is a mind perfectly disembodied. It does not care where it is so long as its present location yields a greater advantage than any other. It will do anything at all that is necessary, not merely to live, but to aggrandize itself. And it charges its damages indifferently to the public, to nature, and to the future.

The corporate mind at work overthrows all the virtues of the personal mind, or it throws them out of account. The corporate mind knows no affection, no desire that is not greedy, no local or personal loyalty, no sympathy or reverence or gratitude, no temperance or thrift or self-restraint. It does not observe the first responsibility of intelligence, which is to know when you don't know or when you are being unintelligent. Try to imagine an official standing up in the high councils of a global corporation or a great public institution to say, "We have grown too big," or "We now have more power than we can responsibly use," or "We must treat our employees as our neighbors," or "We must count ourselves as members of this community," or "We must preserve the ecological integrity of our work places," or "Let us do unto others as we would have them to do unto us"—and you will see what I mean.

The corporate mind, on the contrary, justifies and encourages the personal mind in its worst faults and weaknesses, such as greed and servility, and frees it of any need to worry about long-term consequences. For these reliefs, nowadays, the corporate mind is apt to express noisily its gratitude to God.

But now I must hasten to acknowledge that there are some corporations that do not simply incorporate what I am calling the corporate mind. Whether the number of these is increasing or not, I don't know. These organizations, I believe, tend to have hometowns and to count themselves as participants in the local economy and as members of the local community.

-------------◆-------------

I would not apply to science any stricture that I would not apply to the arts, but science now calls for special attention because it has contributed so largely to modern abuses of the natural world, and because of its enormous prestige. Our concern here has to do immediately with the complacency of many scientists. It cannot be denied that science, in its inevitable applications, has given unprecedented extremes of scale to the technologies of land use, manufacturing, and war, and to their bad effects. One response to the manifest implication of science in certain kinds of destruction is to say that we need more science, or more and better science. I am inclined to honor this proposition, if I am allowed to add that we also need more than science.

But I am not at all inclined to honor the proposition that "science is self-correcting" when it implies that science is thus made somehow "safe." Science is no more safe than any other kind of knowledge. And especially it is not safe in the context of its gigantic applications by the corporate mind. Nor is it safe in the context of its own progressivist optimism. The idea, common enough among the universities and their ideological progeny, that one's work, whatever it is, will be beneficently disposed by the market or the hidden hand or evolution or some other obscure force is an example of counterfeit knowledge.

The obvious immediate question is, How *soon* can science correct itself? Can it correct itself soon enough to prevent or correct the real damage of its errors? The answer is that it cannot correct itself soon enough. Scientists who have made a plausible "breakthrough" hasten to tell the world, including of course the corporations. And while science may have corrected itself, it is not necessarily able to correct its results or its influence.

We must grant of course that science in its laboratories may be well under control. Scientists in laboratories did not cause the ozone hole or the hypoxic zones or acid rain or Chernobyl or Bhopal or Love Canal. It is when knowledge is corporatized, commercialized, and applied that it goes out of control. Can science, then, make itself responsible by issuing appropriate warnings with its knowledge? No, because the users are under no obligation to heed or respect the warning. If the knowledge is conformable to the needs of profit or power, the warning will be ignored, as we know. We are not excused by the doctrine of scientific self-correction from worrying about the influence of science on the corporate mind, and about the influence of the corporate mind on the minds of consumers and users. Humans in general have got to worry about the origins of the permission we have given ourselves to do large-scale damage. That permission is our problem, for by it we have made our ignorance arrogant and given it immeasurable power to do harm. We are killing our world on the theory that it was never alive but is only an accidental concatenation of materials and mechanical processes. We are killing one another and ourselves on the same theory. If life has no standing as mystery or miracle or gift, then what signifies the difference between it and death?

To state the problem more practically, we can say that the ignorant use of knowledge allows power to override the question of scale, because it overrides respect for the integrity of local ecosystems, which respect alone can determine the appropriate scale of human work. Without propriety of scale, and the acceptance of limits which that implies, there can be no form—and here we reunite science and art. We live and prosper by form, which is the power of creatures and artifacts to be made whole within their proper limits. Without formal restraints, power necessarily becomes inordinate and destructive. This is why the poet David Jones wrote in the midst of World War II that "man as artist hungers and thirsts after form." Inordinate size has of itself the power to exclude much knowledge.

------------◆------------

What can we do? Anybody who goes on so long about a problem is rightly expected to have something to say about a solution. One is expected to "end on a positive note," and I mean to do that. But I also mean to be careful. The question, What can we do? especially when the problem is large, implies the expectation of a large solution.

I have no large solution to offer. There is, as maybe we all have noticed, a conspicuous shortage of large-scale corrections for problems that have large-scale causes. Our damages to watersheds and ecosystems will have to be corrected one farm, one forest, one acre at a time. The aftermath of a bombing has to be dealt with one corpse, one wound at a time. And so the first temptation to avoid is the call for some sort of revolution. To imagine that destructive power might be made harmless by gathering enough power to destroy it is of course perfectly futile. William Butler Yeats said as much in his poem "The Great Day":

> Hurrah for revolution and more cannon shot!
> A beggar upon horseback lashes a beggar on foot.
> Hurrah for revolution and cannon come again!
> The beggars have changed places, but the lash goes on.

Arrogance cannot be cured by greater arrogance, or ignorance by greater ignorance. To counter the ignorant use of knowledge and power we have, I am afraid, only a proper humility, and this is laughable. But it is only partly laughable. In his political pastoral "Build Soil," as if responding to Yeats, Robert Frost has one of his rustics say,

> I bid you to a one-man revolution—
> The only revolution that is coming.

If we find the consequences of our arrogant ignorance to be humbling, and we are humbled, then we have at hand the first fact of hope: We can change ourselves. We, each of us severally, can remove our minds from the corporate ignorance and arrogance that is leading the world to destruction; we can honestly confront our ignorance and our need; we can take guidance from the knowledge we most authentically possess, from experience, from tradition, and from the inward promptings of affection, conscience, decency, compassion, even inspiration.

This change can be called by several names—change of heart, rebirth, metanoia, enlightenment—and it belongs, I think, to all the religions, but I like the practical way it is defined in the Confucian *Great Digest*. This is from Ezra Pound's translation:

> The men of old wanting to clarify and diffuse throughout the
> empire that light which comes from looking straight into the
> heart and then acting, first set up good government in their own

states; wanting good government in their states, they first established order in their own families; wanting order in the home,
they first disciplined themselves; desiring self-discipline, they
rectified their own hearts; and wanting to rectify their hearts,
they sought precise verbal definitions of their inarticulate
thoughts [the tones given off by the heart]; wishing to attain
precise verbal definitions, they set to extend their knowledge to
the utmost.

This curriculum does not rule out science—it does not rule out knowledge
of any kind—but it begins with the recognition of ignorance and of need,
of being in a bad situation.

---------◆---------

If the ability to change oneself is the first fact of hope, then the second surely
must be an honest assessment of the badness of our situation. Our situation is extremely bad, as I have said, and optimism cannot either improve
it or make it look better. But there is hope in seeing it as it is. And here I
need to quote Kathleen Raine again. This is a passage written in the aftermath of World War II, and she is thinking of T. S. Eliot's poem *The Waste
Land*, written in the aftermath of World War I. In *The Waste Land*, Eliot bears
unflinching witness to the disease of our time: We are living the death of
our culture and our world. The poem's ruling metaphor is that of a water-
less land perishing for rain, an image that becomes more poignant as we
pump down the aquifers and dry up or pollute the rivers.

> But Eliot [Kathleen Raine said] has shown us what the world is
> very apt to forget, that the statement of a terrible truth has a kind
> of healing power. In his stern vision of the hell that lies about
> us…, there is a quality of grave consolation. In his statement of
> the worst, Eliot has always implied the whole extent of the real-
> ity of which that worst is only one part.

Honesty is good, then, not just because it is a virtue, but for a practical reason: It can give us an accurate description of our problem, and it can set the problem precisely in its context.

Honesty, of course, is not a solution. As I have already said, I don't think there are solutions commensurate with our problems. I think the great problems call for many small solutions. But for that possibility to attain sufficient standing among us, we need not only to put the problems in context but also to learn to put our work in context. And here is where we turn back from our ambitions to consult both the local ecosystem and the cultural instructions conveyed to us by religion and the arts. All the arts and sciences need to be made answerable to standards higher than those of any art or science. Scientists and artists must understand that they can honor their gifts and fulfill their obligations only by living and working as human beings and community members rather than as specialists. What this may involve may not be predictable even by scientists. But the best advice may have been given by Hippocrates: "As to diseases make a habit of two things—to help, or at least, to do no harm."

The wish to help, especially if it is profitable to do so, may be in human nature, and everybody wants to be a hero. To help, or to try to help, requires only knowledge; one needs to know promising remedies and how to apply them. But to do no harm involves a whole culture, and a culture very different from industrialism. It involves, at the minimum, compassion and humility and caution. The person who will undertake to help without doing harm is going to be a person of some complexity, not easily pleased, probably not a hero, probably not a billionaire.

The corporate approach to agriculture or manufacturing or medicine or war increasingly undertakes to help at the risk of harm, sometimes of great harm. And once the risk of harm is appraised as "acceptable," the result often is absurdity: We destroy a village in order to save it; we destroy freedom in order to save it; we destroy the world in order to live in it.

The apostles of the corporate mind say, with a large implicit compliment to themselves, that you cannot succeed without risking failure. And they allude to such examples as that of the Wright brothers. They don't see that the issue of risk raises directly the issue of scale. Risk, like everything else, has an appropriate scale. By propriety of scale we limit the possible damages of the risks we take. If we cannot control scale so as to limit the effects, then we should not take the risk. From this, it is clear that some risks simply should not be taken. Some experiments should not be made. If a Wright brother wishes to risk failure, then he observes a fundamental decency in risking it alone. If the Wright airplane had crashed into a house and killed a child, the corporate mind, considering the future profitability of aviation, would count that an "acceptable" risk and loss. One can only reply that the corporate mind does not have the householder's or the parent's point of view.

--------◆--------

I am aware that invoking personal decency, personal humility, as the solution to a vast risk taken on our behalf by corporate industrialism is not going to suit everybody. Some will find it an insult to their sense of proportion, others to their sense of drama. I am offended by it myself, and I wish I could do better. But having looked about, I have been unable to convince myself that there is a better solution or one that has a better chance of working.

I am trying to follow what T. S. Eliot called "the way of ignorance," for I think that is the way that is appropriate for the ignorant. I think Eliot meant us to understand that the way of ignorance is the way recommended by all the great teachers. It was certainly the way recommended by Confucius, for who but the ignorant would set out to extend their knowledge to the utmost? Who but the knowingly ignorant would know there is an "utmost" to knowledge?

But we take the way of ignorance also as a courtesy toward reality. Eliot wrote in "East Coker":

> The knowledge imposes a pattern, and falsifies,
> For the pattern is new in every moment
> And every moment is a new and shocking
> Valuation of all we have been.

This certainly describes the ignorance inherent in the human condition, an ignorance we justly feel as tragic. But it also is a way of acknowledging the uniqueness of every individual creature, deserving respect, and the uniqueness of every moment, deserving wonder. Life in time involves a great freshness that is falsified by what we already know.

And of course the way of ignorance is the way of faith. If enough of us will accept "the wisdom of humility," giving due honor to the ever-renewing pattern, accepting each moment's "new and shocking/Valuation of all we have been," then the corporate mind as we now have it will be shaken, and it will cease to exist as its members dissent and withdraw from it.

(2004)

The Purpose of a Coherent Community*

I KNOW WELL that I am hardly the first aging man to look back on his youth as "a better time," and perhaps I am sufficiently aware of the dangers. It is true nevertheless that in my lifetime I have witnessed a lot of destruction. And I can't say that I believe this destruction has been compensated by any of the gains we designate as "progress." I think that when the accounts are finally balanced they will show a net loss. I can't forget, for example, that in the time of my childhood people in my part of the world drank fearlessly from springs and wells and swam without anxiety in whatever water was deep enough. We probably should have worried (a little) about coliform and other bacteria, but the possibility of contamination by persistent chemicals did not yet exist for us in that time and place.

Now, of course, we know that water pollution is only a part of a package that includes air pollution, soil erosion, deforestation, urban sprawl, architectural ugliness, and other symptoms of a general disregard for the world's life and health. Now we not only cannot drink fearlessly from wells and springs; we cannot drink fearlessly from the public plumbing; we cannot fearlessly breathe the air.

Here is a set of sentences culled from a book I wish were better known:

> We have been greatly engaged in digging up the stored re-
> sources, and in destroying vast products of the earth for some

*Written originally as a speech delivered on September 29, 2004, to the National Preservation Conference of the National Trust for Historic Preservation at Louisville, Kentucky.

small kernel that we can apply to our necessities or add to our enjoyments. We...blast the minerals and the metals from underneath the crust and leave the earth raw and sore...exterminate whole races of animals; choke the streams with refuse and dross; rob the land of its available stores, denuding the surface, exposing great areas to erosion.

. . .

...those who appropriate the accumulations of the earth should complete their work, cleaning up the remainders, leaving the areas wholesome, inoffensive, and safe.

. . .

Yet there is even a more defenseless devastation...It is the organized destructiveness of those who would make military domination the major premise in the constitution of society, accompanying desolation with viciousness and violence...disrespecting the works of the creator...

. . .

Today we are moved by impulses of trade, and we find ourselves plunged into a war of commercial frenzy...Rivalry that leads to arms is a natural fruit of unrestrained rivalry in trade.

. . .

...we have taken [the earth] for granted ... and with little care or conscious thought of the consequences of our use of it.

If those grief-stricken sentences sound familiar, that is not because they are contemporary. They were written in the first year of World War I by Liberty Hyde Bailey, the great dean, by then retired, of the College of Agriculture at Cornell University. Those sentences become even more poignant for a person today who reads on in that little book, *The Holy Earth*, because the next chapter sets forth the belief that we were then at the beginning of a new era in our use of the land, when we would waste little and do no harm, when farming would cease to be "a mining process" and become "really productive and constructive." But since Dean Bailey died at ninety-six in 1954, something like one-third of the world's farmable soil has been lost to erosion; we have brought clearly into sight the end of the era of cheap fossil fuels; we have polluted the entire earth with our poisons; and wars of commercial frenzy, raging on and on, have apparently been accepted by our officials as a sort of economic norm. Since 1954 most of our towns and cities have become formless, decadent, and ugly; and huge expanses of our fertile countryside have become monocultural deserts, toxic, depopulated, and ugly.

---------◆---------

As signs, or perhaps symptoms, of the general destructiveness of the industrial economy, we now have hundreds of large and small organizations devoted to protecting or saving things of value that are endangered: peace, kindness, freedom, childhood, health, wilderness areas, rivers, species of plants and animals, cultures, languages, farmland, family farms, farm families, families, the atmosphere, scenic roads, fine old buildings, historic places, holy places, quietness, darkness. More and more, as I tell over our lengthening catalog of calamities and discouragements, I think of these organizations. I think of them with great sympathy, and with love, for I think they are the basis of our worldly hope. They are the basis of our *right* to hope that our own greatly endangered species may somehow be saved, if not from extinction, at least from the necessity of recognizing itself as the ultimate parasite, deserving extinction.

Collectively, these organizations comprise a movement of redemption, a movement to deliver the holy earth from its ruthless exploiters who are claiming everywhere their "right" to plunder, waste, corrupt, and destroy the great possessions that have been given to us on the condition only of our devoted care. I believe that the people in these organizations understand, or they are beginning to understand, the propriety of Dean Bailey's phrase "the holy earth." For at present there is nothing, literally nothing, that is held sacred by the proponents of so-called development.

These many redemptive organizations are now required to confront consciously and capably, really for the first time in human history, a question that is almost overwhelming in its magnitude and urgency but also is utterly fascinating, fully worthy of a lifetime's effort and study: Can we change the ways we live and work so as to establish a preserving harmony between the made and the given worlds? Or, to make that question more practical and immediate: Can great power or great wealth be kind to small places? Can the necessary industries subsist upon their natural sources without destroying them? Can the life of a farm or working forest be made compatible with its local ecosystem? Can city and country live and trade together to their mutual benefit? Can an urban economy vouchsafe the health and prosperity of its suppliers, its consumers, and its neighbors? One takes much hope and encouragement from the knowledge that everywhere in our country and in the world, thanks to these organizations, people in significant numbers are beginning to suffer these questions.

————◆————

And yet, grateful as I am for these organizations, so many of whose names begin with "Save," I can't help but notice that this movement or this consciousness that I am calling redemptive, and am moreover a part of, is not only the losing side in our current public struggles, but in terms of its standing and influence is hardly a side at all. It doesn't have a significant political presence. It is virtually unrepresented in our state and federal governments. Most of its concerns are not on the agenda of either major party. It is now impossible to imagine a major politician standing up in public and asking, Why are so many irreplaceable things, from mountains to memories, being destroyed by so-called economic development? Why are so many things we need, from healthy farms to health, being priced out of existence by the so-called free market?

No major politician is asking such questions because no major politician is adequately supported by a constituency that is asking such questions.

The constituency exists, I believe, or at least the beginning of it does, in all those precious organizations that I have been praising. And so I need to add to my praise some criticism, not in disparagement but in hope, for when we try to think of those organizations all together as a constituency we see that, as such, it is badly disintegrated and fragmented. Its efforts are scattered, often mutually exclusive, sometimes mutually competitive, and mostly negative. In some of its parts, it is fearful of becoming too radical. For the purpose of its own coherence, it is not radical enough.

It is immensely heartening to know that the National Trust is interested in coherence and so can devote itself to such multiple purposes as "the preservation and restoration of buildings and landscapes," can propose "to save historic places and revitalize communities," and can see "historic preservation as a tool for restoring economic vitality to traditional business districts." But even within and among those excellent aims there is trouble.

If, for example, you are interested in the preservation and restoration of landscapes, you will find out quickly that there are, with us, two classes of landscapes: the would-be pristine landscapes of parks and wilderness preserves, and the economic landscapes of farms and working forests. The conservationists and the land users who seek to preserve those landscapes, though they have many of the same enemies and many reasons to be allies, have a long history of mutual enmity and dislike (see Courtney White's essay, p. 159).

Or if you are interested in restoring economic vitality to traditional business districts in our town and urban centers, you will find an even more complicated muddle. Businesses, with us, are of two kinds: locally-owned businesses that are relatively small, and national or supranational corporations. The interests of these kinds of businesses are almost diametrically opposed, and yet the local business people, who everywhere are being destroyed by the great corporations, are all too likely to believe that their interests are the same—and, at the same time, are all too likely to be antipathetic to the rural land users and the conservationists who are their natural allies.

----------◆----------

Even a great redemptive effort, under way nearly everywhere and supported by the good work of many people, when it is as scattered and dis-
connected as this one, is almost inevitably going to be mostly negative.
Among the many organizations I am talking about, the most popular
words, after "save," are "stop" and "no." Even the preservation of something
of value is negative if it reduces the possibility of preserving something
else of value.

It is, of course, perfectly all right to be against something that is wrong.
If we see that something is wrong we have no choice but to oppose it—for
the sake, if for nothing else, of our own souls. And yet, in so destructive an
age as ours, it is possible for our sense of wrong to become an affliction. All
of us who are committed to saving things of value have been in what Wes
Jackson calls "the ain't-it-awful conversation," in which we recite the current litany of outrages. We have been in that conversation, and, if we have
brought to it a modicum of sanity, we have recognized sooner or later the
need to get out of it. The logical end of the ain't-it-awful conversation, as of
the life devoted merely to opposition, is despair. People quit having any
fun, they begin to talk about the "inevitability" of what they are against,
and they give up. Mere opposition finally blinds us to the good of the things
we are trying to save. And it divides us hopelessly from our opponents, who
no doubt are caricaturing us while we are demonizing them. We lose, in
short, the sense of shared humanity that would permit us to say even to our
worst enemies, "We are working, after all, in your interest and your children's. Ours is a common effort for the common good. Come and join us."

----------◆----------

That this redemptive movement is not yet seen clearly enough, even by the
people in it, as a common effort for the common good is perfectly understandable. Undoubtedly it began in the only way it could have begun. Its
many organizations have necessarily defined themselves by the singular
problems they have addressed:

"The river is being polluted. Save the river. Stop pollution. No to the polluters."

"We are losing our architectural inheritance. Save the inner city. Stop the demolition. No to the wreckers."

This is clear enough. If we are sympathetic, the only possible objection is that it is incomplete; it does not go far enough. The effort is not only defined by the problem but is limited by it. An effort that is defined only or mainly by a problem is negative necessarily. And under the rhetoric of Save and Stop and No there lies an odd and embarrassing fact. Who is polluting the river? Well, among others, *we* are, we members of Save the River, who flush our toilets and use the latest toxic products only a little less thoughtlessly than everybody else. Who is wrecking the inner city? *We* are, of course, we members of Save the Inner City, who drive our cars and shop at the malls and the chain stores only a little less thoughtlessly than everybody else. It doesn't make any difference that we mostly don't have an alternative to doing as we do; we still share the guilt. In a centralized, specialized, commercialized, mechanized society such as ours, we all are necessarily, and in considerable measure, helping to cause the problems we are helping to deplore and trying to solve.

I would be wrong, at this point, if I failed to notice that our side, this redemptive movement compounded of so many aims and efforts, has won a good many victories, and we are right to rejoice in them and take courage from them. But these victories, I am afraid, are isolated. They don't yet constitute a significant pattern or tendency of cultural change. We have won victories, but we still are losing.

————◆————

If our efforts are fragmented and our victories are piecemeal, then clearly we have got to think again and think better. In order to think better, I believe, we are going to have to revive and reinvigorate the tired old idea of context. A creature can live only in a context that favors its life. An artifact exists and means only in a context that supports it and reinforces its meaning.

The people who can most usefully instruct us about context are the ecologists, who have most usefully instructed us about habitat. If we want to preserve a species, then we have got to preserve its habitat. Its habitat is comprised of the local soil, topography, climate, and community of creatures, but ultimately its habitat is the world's one atmosphere and its one hydrologic cycle. The context of everything is everything else.

There is no escape from the issue of context, and if we think of modern life in terms of context we are going to find it abounding in inconsistencies, and in moral discomforts that we have taught ourselves not to feel. Here are some examples:

If we can't preserve the health of the natural world in our economic landscapes of farm and ranch and working forest, and even in our cities, then we are not going to be able to preserve it in our parks and wilderness preserves.

To countenance mountain removal in Kentucky and West Virginia is to agree to the eventual destruction of Yosemite and Yellowstone and the Smokies.

We can't for long preserve the fine arts if we neglect or destroy the domestic arts of farming, forestry, cooking, clothing, building, homemaking, community life, and local economy.

We can't talk to any purpose about the "beauty" of religious art and architecture if we hold religion categorically in contempt.

We can't preserve alive the great poems and stories, as Kathleen Raine wrote, "in the context of a culture not only unlike, but in its fundamental premises opposed to" the cultures that produced them.

We can't preserve historic buildings to any purpose or for very long outside the contexts of community life and local economy.

In short, we can't preserve the best of human and earthly life merely as a museum of obsolete artifacts, rare creatures, and unusual scenery.

The most forceful context of every habitat now is the industrial economy that is doing damage to all habitats. We can't preserve neighborliness or charity or peaceability or an ecological consciousness, or anything else worth preserving, at the same time that we maintain an earth-destroying economy. Nothing ultimately flourishes in our present economy but selfish aims, and these are often mutually contradictory. We have to have a sort of pity for the CEO of a polluting corporation who desires wealth, healthy children, and a vacation in the restorative purity of nature. And surely we have to extend the same pity to those who are sure that "it takes a village to raise a child" but who forget that it takes a local culture and a local economy to raise a village.

Contradictions so obvious and so ordinary alert us to the importance of preserving or advocating a whole thing. We have too many reasons to suspect that even the most valuable things cannot be preserved, or not for long, merely by the desire to save them, or even by the necessary money, or even by the necessary votes. And so let us say that a whole thing is anything worth preserving plus its preserving context. Let us call the preserving context a community, for that is the name of the having-in-common that does in fact preserve us. And let us understand that we must never allow our thoughts or wishes to separate the community from its habitat, or from its economy, which is its way of living in its habitat, or from its culture, which is its way of remembering (or forgetting) where it is and how to live there.

We seem to have been living for a long time on the assumption that we can safely deal with parts, leaving the whole to take care of itself. But now the news from everywhere is that we have to begin gathering up the scattered pieces, figuring out where they belong, and putting them back together. For the parts can be reconciled to one another only within the pattern of the whole thing to which they belong. The local business people, farmers, foresters, conservationists, investors, bankers, and builders are not going to get along on the basis of economic determinism. The ground of their reconciliation will have to be larger than the ground of their divisions. It will have to promise life, satisfaction, and hope to them all.

The common denominator is the local community. Only the purpose of a coherent community, fully alive both in the world and in the minds of its members, can carry us beyond fragmentation, contradiction, and negativity, teaching us to preserve, not in opposition but in affirmation and affection, all things needful to make us glad to live.

--------◆--------

A coherent community is undoubtedly an excellent purpose. Perhaps we can agree that it is. But we will have to agree also, I am afraid, that none of us lives in one, and that none of us knows where to find one—unless it might be one of the older Amish communities, which we would find to be instructive but also in many ways dependent on our own disintegrating society. History provides many examples of coherent communities, but not one that we can "go back to." We have no place to begin but where we are.

Where we are is a world dominated by a global economy that places no value whatsoever on community or community coherence. In this economy, whose business is to set in contention things that belong together, you can do nothing more divisive than to assert the claims of community. This puts you immediately at odds with powerful people to whom the claims of community mean nothing, who ignore the issues of locality, who recognize no neighbors and are loyal to no place. These people believe, as W. Michael Cox and Richard Alm wrote in the *New York Times* of November 7, 2003, that "microeconomic failure"—by which they mean loss of jobs, displacement of workers, and the disruption of communities—is necessary for "macroeconomic" progress. Such failure, they wrote, "is the way the macro economy transfers resources to where they belong." We must not object to microeconomic failure, these writers said, because "Large-scale upheaval in jobs is part of the economy…History tells us that the result will be even more jobs, greater productivity and higher incomes for American workers in general."

We are indebted to Mr. Cox and Mr. Alm for telling us so precisely what we are up against. If the claims of community are to be asserted now, they must be asserted in the face of this heartless optimism backed by the world's wealth and power, and with virtually all the world's people as its dependents.

Putting the pieces back together is going to be slow work. The pieces can be scattered in a hurry merely by indifference or neglect or violence. But the same forces that scattered them cannot put them back together. For that, we are going to need the hope and the purpose of a coherent community, clearly articulated and steadily borne in mind. And we are going to have to resign ourselves to patience and small steps.

We are indebted to Mr. Cox and Mr. Alm also for displaying in blatant outline the great fault of their thesis. That fault is in their debasement of vocation to "job," implying that what a worker does or where it is done does not matter so long as the worker gets paid for doing it. Their reduction of vocation to "job" leads necessarily to their further reduction of working people to "resources," not different in kind or value from raw materials or machine parts.

To this, the purpose of a coherent community gives us the necessary answer, which is at the same time the means of unifying and making politically effective our now disparate efforts to save the good things: The members of a community cohere on the basis of their recognized need for one another, a need that is in many ways practical but never utilitarian. The members of a coherent community, moreover, keep the good things they have because of a recognized need for them, a need sufficiently practical but never utilitarian.

If it is to cohere, a community cannot agree to the loss of any of its members, or the disemployment of any of its members, as an acceptable cost of an economic program. If it is to cohere, a community must remember its history and its obligations; it is therefore irreconcilably opposed to "mobility" as a social norm. Persons, places, and things have a practical value, but they are not reducible to such value; they are not interchangeable. That is why we outlawed slavery. That is why a house for sale is not a home.

(2004)

Quantity vs. Form*

―――――――――――――――――――――――

I

MY FAMILY AND I had a good friend I will call Lily. Lily was industrious and generous, a good neighbor. She was especially well-loved by her neighbors' children and grandchildren, though she had no children of her own. She lived a long time, surviving her husband by many years. At last, permanently ill and debilitated, she had to leave the small house that she and her husband had bought in their latter years and go to the nursing home. My brother, who was her lawyer, never until then much needed, arranged for the sale of her house and all her worldly goods.

I went to visit her a day or two after the sale. She was bedfast, sick and in some pain, but perfectly clear in her mind. We talked of the past and of several of our old neighbors, long gone. And then, speaking of the sale of her possessions, she said, "I'm all finished now. Everything is done."

She said this so cheerfully that I asked her, "Lily, is it a load off your mind?"

She said, "Well, Wendell, it hurt me. I laid here the night when I knew it was all gone, and I could *see* it all, all the things I'd cared for so long. But, yes, it is a load off my mind."

I was so moved and impressed by what she said that I wrote it down. She had lived her life and met her hardships bravely and cheerfully, and now she faced her death fully aware and responsible and with what seemed to me a completed grace. I didn't then and I don't now see how she could have been more admirable.

*Written originally for a conference, "Evidence-Based, Opinion-Based, and Real World Agriculture and Medicine," convened by Charlie Sing at Emigrant, Montana, October 10–15, 2004.

The last time I saw Lily she was in the hospital, where the inevitable course of her illness had taken her. By then, in addition to a seriously afflicted heart, she had not recovered from a bout of pneumonia, and because of osteoporosis she had several broken bones. She was as ill probably as a living creature can be and in great pain. She was dying. But in talking with the resident physician, I discovered that he had taken her off her pain medication to increase her appetite in the hope, he said, of "getting her back on her feet."

And so a life in every sense complete had to suffer at its end this addendum of useless and meaningless pain. I don't think this episode is unusual or anomalous at the present time. The doctor's stupidity and cowardice are in fact much mitigated by being perfectly conventional. The medical industry now instructs us all that longevity is a good in itself. Plain facts and simple mercy, moreover, are readily obscured by the supposed altruism of the intent to "heal."

I am obliged now to say that I am by no means an advocate of euthanasia or "assisted suicide." My purpose here is only to notice that the ideal of a whole or a complete life, as expressed in Psalm 128 or in Tiresias' foretelling of the death of Odysseus, now appears to have been replaced by the ideal merely of a *long* life. And I do not believe that these two ideals can be reconciled.

As a man growing old, I have not been able to free my mind of the story of Lily's last days or of other stories like it that I know, and I have not been able to think of them without fear. This fear is only somewhat personal. It is also a cultural fear, the fear that something valuable and necessary to our life is being lost.

--------◆--------

To clarify my thoughts I have been in need of some further example, and recently the associations of reading led me to Robert Southey's account of the Battle of Trafalgar in his biography of Lord Nelson. I am by conviction a pacifist, but that does not prevent me from being moved and instructed by the story of a military hero. What impresses me in Southey's account is the substantial evidence that Nelson went into the battle both expecting and fully prepared to die.

He expected to die because he had refused any suggestion that he should enter the battle in disguise in order to save himself. Instead, he would wear, Southey wrote, "as usual, his Admiral's frockcoat, bearing on the left breast four stars of the different orders with which he was invested." He thus made himself the prime target of the engagement; he would live and fight as himself, though it meant that he would die unmistakably as himself. As for his decorations: "In honor I gained them, and in honor I will die with them." And before the battle he wrote out a prayer, asking for a British victory but also for humanity afterward toward the enemy. "For myself individually," he wrote, "I commit my life to Him who made me…"

At the end of his account, published in 1813, eight years after the battle, Southey wrote of the admiral's death a verdict undoubtedly not so remarkable then as the succeeding two centuries have made it: "There was reason to suppose, from the appearance upon opening the body, that in the course of nature he might have attained, like his father, to a good old age. Yet he cannot be said to have fallen prematurely whose work was done…"

Nelson was killed at the age of forty-seven, which would seem to us in our time to be a life cut "tragically short." But Southey credited to that life a formal completeness that had little to do with its extent and much to do with its accomplishments and with Nelson's own sense of its completeness: "Thank God, I have done my duty."

--------◆--------

The issue of the form of a lived life is difficult, for the form as opposed to the measurable extent of a life has as much to do with inward consciousness as with verifiable marks left on the world. But we are already in the thick of the problem when we have noticed that there does seem to be such a thing as a good life; that a good life consists, in part at least, of doing well; and that this possibility is an ancient one, having apparently little to do with the progress of science or how much a person knows. And so we must ask how it is that one does not have to know everything in order to do well.

The answer, apparently, is that one does so by accepting formal constraints. We are excused from the necessity of creating the universe, and most of us will not have even to command a fleet in a great battle. We come to form, we in-form our lives, by accepting the obvious limits imposed by our talents and circumstances, by nature and mortality, and thus by getting the scale right. Form permits us to live and work gracefully within our limits.

In *The Soil and Health*, his light-giving book of 1947, Sir Albert Howard wrote:

> It needs a more refined perception to recognize throughout this stupendous wealth of varying shapes and forms the principle of stability. Yet this principle dominates. It dominates by means of an ever-recurring cycle, a cycle which, repeating itself silently and ceaselessly, ensures the continuation of living matter. This cycle is constituted of the successive and repeated processes of birth, growth, maturity, death, and decay.

Following, as he said, "an eastern religion," Howard speaks of this cycle as "The Wheel of Life." The life of nature depends upon the uninterrupted turning of this wheel. Howard's work rested upon his conviction, obviously correct, that a farm needed to incorporate within its own working the entire revolution of the wheel of life, so that it too might remain endlessly alive and productive by obeying "Nature's law of return." When, thirty years ago, I wrote in a poem, "The farm is an infinite form," this is what I meant.

The wheel of life is a form. It is a natural form, and it can become an artistic form insofar as the art of farming and the work of a farm can be made to conform to it. It can be made a form also of the art of living, but that, I think, requires an additional step. The wheel of human—that is, of *fully* human—life would consist over the generations of birth, growth, maturity, *ripeness*, death, and decay.

"Ripeness" is implicit in the examples of Lord Nelson and my friend Lily, but the term itself comes from act V, scene 2, of *King Lear*, in which Edgar says to his father:

> Men must endure
> Their going hence, even as their coming hither.
> Ripeness is all.

By "ripeness" Edgar means a perfect readiness for death, and his sentence echoes "The readiness is all" in act V, scene 2, of *Hamlet*. In the wheel of human life, "ripeness" adds to the idea of biological growth the growth in a living soul of the knowledge of time and eternity in preparation for death. And after the addition of "ripeness," "decay" acquires the further sense of the "plowing in" of experience and memory, building up the cultural humus. The art of living thus is practiced not only by individuals, but by whole communities or societies. It is the work of the long-term education of a people. Its purpose, we may say, is to make life conform gracefully both to its natural course and to its worldly limits. And this is in fulfillment of what Vermont Chief Justice Jeffrey L. Amestoy says is "our common responsibility…to imagine humanity the heart can recognize."

———————◆———————

What is or what should be the goal of our life and work? This is a fearful question and it ought to be fearfully answered. Probably it should not be answered for anybody in particular by anybody else in particular. But the ancient norm or ideal seems to have been a life in which you perceived your calling, faithfully followed it, and did your work with satisfaction; married, made a home, and raised a family; associated generously with neighbors; ate and drank with pleasure the produce of your local landscape; grew old seeing yourself replaced by your children or younger neighbors, but continuing in old age to be useful; and finally died a good or a holy death surrounded by loved ones.

Now we seem to have lost any such thought of a completed life. We no longer imagine death as an appropriate end or as a welcome deliverance from pain or grief or weariness. Death now apparently is understood, and especially by those who have placed themselves in charge of it, as a punishment for growing old, to be delayed at any cost.

We seem to be living now with the single expectation that there should and will always be more of everything, including "life expectancy." This insatiable desire for more is the result of an overwhelming sense of incompleteness, which is the result of the insatiable desire for more. This is the wheel of death. It is the revolving of this wheel that now drives technological progress. The more superficial and unsatisfying our lives become, the faster we need to progress. When you are skating on thin ice, speed up.

The medical industry's invariable unction about life-saving, healing, and the extended life expectancy badly needs a meeting on open ground with tragedy, absurdity, and moral horror. To wish for a longer life is to wish implicitly for an extension of the possibility that one's life may become a burden or even a curse. And what are we to think when a criminal becomes a medical emergency by the beneficence of nature, is accorded the full panoply of technological mercy, and is soon back in practice? The moral horror comes when the suffering or dementia of an overly extended life is reduced to another statistical verification of the "miracle" of modern medicine; or when a mental disease, such as the inability to face death or an ungovernable greed for more of everything, is exploited for profit.

Perhaps there is nobody now who has not benefited in some urgently personal way from the technology of the modern medical industry. To disregard the benefit is a falsehood, and to be ungrateful is inexcusable. But even gratitude does not free us of the obligation to be critical when criticism is needed. And there can be no doubt that the rapid development of industrial technology in medicine—and, as I am about to show, in agriculture—is much in need of criticism. We need to study with great concern the effects of introducing the mechanical and chemical procedures and quantitative standards of industry into the organic world and into the care of creatures. If this has given us benefits, it has also charged us and our world with costs that, typically, have been ignored by the accountants of progress. There is never, at best, an exact fit between the organic world and industrial technology. At worst, there is contradiction, opposition, and serious damage.

Industrial technology tends to obscure or destroy the sense of appropriate scale and of propriety of application. The standard of performance tends to be set by the capacity of the technology rather than the individual nature of places and creatures. Industrial technology, instead of adapting itself to life, attempts to adapt life to itself by treating life as merely a mechanical or chemical process, and thus it inhibits the operation of love, imagination, familiarity, compassion, fear, and awe. It reduces responsibility to routine, and work to "processing." It destroys the worker's knowledge of what is being worked upon.

II

THE OPPOSITION OF QUANTITY and form in agriculture is not so immediately painful as in medicine, but it is more obvious. The medical industry has lifted the "norm" of life expectancy out of reach by proposing to extend longevity ad infinitum. Likewise, agricultural science, agribusiness, and the food industry propose to increase production ad infinitum, and this is their only aim. They will increase production by any means and at any cost, even at the cost of future productivity, for they have no functioning idea of ecological or agricultural or human limits. And since the agricultural economy is controlled by agribusiness and the food industry, their fixation on quantity is too easily communicated to farmers.

The art of farming, as I said earlier, fashions the farm's cycle of productivity so that it conforms to the wheel of life. That is Sir Albert Howard's language. In Wes Jackson's language, the art of farming is to mimic on the farm the self-renewing processes of the local ecosystem. But that is not all. The art of farming is also the art of living on a farm. The form of a farm is partly in its embodied consciousness of ecological obligation, and thus in its annual cycle of work, but it is also in the arrangement of fields and buildings in relation to the life of the farm's human family whose focus is the household. There is thus a convergence or even a coincidence between the form of a farm and the form of a farming life. The art of sustaining fertility and the art of living on a farm are mutually enhancing and mutually reinforcing.

A long view of an old agricultural landscape, in America and even more in Europe, would show how fencerows and fields have conformed over time both to natural topography and to human use, and how the location of dwellings, barns, and outbuildings reveals the established daily and seasonal patterns of work. In talking now about such farms in such landscapes, we are talking mostly about the past. Such farms were highly diversified and formally complex, and sometimes they were impressively sensitive (though perhaps no farm can ever be sensitive enough) both to the requirements of the place and to human need. The pursuit of higher and higher productivity has replaced those complex forms with the form (if it can be called that) of a straight line. The minimal formality of the straight line is even further attenuated because the line really is an arrow pointing toward nothing at all that is present, but toward the goal of even more production in the future. The line, it is proposed, will go on and on from one record yield to another. And the line of this determination is marked on the ground by longer and longer rows, which is to say larger and larger farms.

The exclusive standard of productivity destroys the formal integrity of a farm just as the exclusive standard of longevity destroys the formal integrity of a life. The quest for higher and higher production on farms leads almost inevitably to specialization, ignoring the natural impulsion toward diversity; specialization in turn obliterates local proprieties of scale and proportion and obscures any sense of human connection. Driven by fashion, debt, and bad science, the desire for more overrides completely the idea of a home or a home place or a home economy or a home community. The desire for quantity replaces the desire for wholeness or holiness or health. The sense of right proportion and scale cannot survive the loss of the sense of relationship, of the parts to one another and to the whole. The result, inevitably, is ugliness, violence, and waste.

Those of us who have watched, and have cared, have seen the old diverse and complex farm homesteads dissolving into an oversimplified, overcapitalized, market-determined agriculture that destroys farms and farmers. The fences, the fencerow plants and animals, the woodlots, the ponds and wetlands, the pastures and hayfields, the grassed waterways all disappear. The farm buildings go from disuse to neglect to decay and finally to fire and the bulldozer. The farmhouse is rented, dishonored, neglected until it too goes down and disappears. A neighborhood of home places, a diverse and comely farmed landscape, is thus replaced by a mechanical and chemical, entirely-patented agricultural desert. And this is a typical reductionist blunder, the success story of a sort of materialist fundamentalism.

By indulging a limitless desire for a supposedly limitless quantity, one gives up all the things that are most desirable. One abandons any hope of the formal completeness, grace, and beauty that come only by subordinating one's life to the whole of which it is a part, and thus one is condemned to the life of a fragment, forever unfinished and incomplete, forever greedy. One loses, that is, the sense of human life as an artifact, a part made imaginatively whole.

(2004)

Renewing Husbandry*

I REMEMBER WELL a summer morning in about 1950 when my father sent a hired man with a McCormick High Gear No. 9 mowing machine and a team of mules to the field I was mowing with our nearly new Farmall A. That memory is a landmark in my mind and my history. I had been born into the way of farming represented by the mule team, and I loved it. I knew irresistibly that the mules were good ones. They were stepping along beautifully at a rate of speed in fact only a little slower than mine. But now I saw them suddenly from the vantage point of the tractor, and I remember how fiercely I resented their slowness. I saw them as "in my way." For those who have had no similar experience, I was feeling exactly the outrage and the low-grade superiority of a hot-rodder caught behind an aged dawdler in urban traffic. It is undoubtedly significant that in the summer of 1950 I passed my sixteenth birthday and became eligible to solve all my problems by driving an automobile.

This is not an exceptional or a remarkably dramatic bit of history. I recite it here to confirm that the industrialization of agriculture is a part of my familiar experience. I don't have the privilege of looking at it as an outsider. It is not incomprehensible to me. The burden of this essay, on the contrary, is that the industrialization of agriculture is a grand oversimplification, too readily comprehensible, to me and to everybody else.

We were mowing that morning, the teamster with his mules and I with the tractor, in the field behind the barn on my father's home place, where

*Written originally as the Klepper Lecture for the Annual Meeting of the Crop Science Society of America in Seattle; delivered on November 2, 2004.

he and before him his father had been born, and where his father had died in February of 1946. The old way of farming was intact in my grandfather's mind until the day he died at eighty-two. He had worked mules all his life, understood them thoroughly, and loved the good ones passionately. He knew tractors only from a distance, he had seen only a few of them, and he rejected them out of hand because he thought, correctly, that they compacted the soil.

Even so, four years after his death his grandson's sudden resentment of the "slow" mule team foretold what history would bear out: The tractor would stay and the mules would go. Year after year, agriculture would be adapted more and more to the technology and the processes of industry and to the rule of industrial economics. This transformation occurred with astonishing speed because, by the measures it set for itself, it was wonderfully successful. It "saved labor," it conferred the prestige of modernity, and it was highly productive.

-------------◆-------------

Though I never entirely departed from farming or at least from thoughts of farming, and my affection for my homeland remained strong, during the fourteen years after 1950 I was much away from home and was not giving to farming the close and continuous attention I have given to it in the forty years since.

In 1964 my family and I returned to Kentucky, and in a year were settled on a hillside farm in my native community, where we have continued to live. Perhaps because I was a returned traveler intending to stay, I now saw the place more clearly than before. I saw it critically, too, for it was evident at once that the human life of the place, the life of the farms and the farming community, was in decline. The old self-sufficient way of farming was passing away. The economic prosperity that had visited the farmers briefly during World War II and for a few years afterward had ended. The little towns that once had been social and economic centers, thronged with country people on Saturdays and Saturday nights, were losing out to the bigger towns and the cities. The rural neighborhoods, once held together by common memories, common work, and the sharing of help, had begun to dissolve. There were no longer local markets for chickens or eggs or cream. The spring lamb industry, once a staple of the region, was gone. The tractors and other mechanical devices certainly were saving the labor of the farmers and farm hands who had moved away, but those who had stayed were working harder and longer than ever.

Because I remembered with affection and respect my grandparents and other country people of their generation, and because I had admirable friends and neighbors with whom I was again farming, I began to ask what was happening, and why. I began to ask what would be the effects on the land, on the community, on the natural world, and on the art of farming. And these questions have occupied me steadily ever since.

The effects of this process of industrialization have become so apparent, so numerous, so favorable to the agribusiness corporations, and so unfavorable to everything else, that by now the questions troubling me and a few others in the 1960s and 1970s are being asked everywhere.

There are no doubt many ways of accounting for this change, but for convenience and brevity I am going to attribute it to the emergence of context as an issue. It has become increasingly clear that the way we farm affects the local community, and that the economy of the local community affects the way we farm; that the way we farm affects the health and integrity of the local ecosystem, and that the farm is intricately dependent, even economically, upon the health of the local ecosystem. We can no longer pretend that agriculture is a sort of economic machine with interchangeable parts, the same everywhere, determined by "market forces" and independent of everything else. We are not farming in a specialist capsule or a professionalist department; we are farming in the world, in a webwork of dependences and influences more intricate than we will ever understand. It has become clear, in short, that we have been running our fundamental economic enterprise by the wrong rules. We were wrong to assume that agriculture could be adequately defined by reductionist science and determinist economics.

If you can keep the context narrow enough (and the accounting period short enough), then the industrial criteria of labor saving and high productivity seem to work well. But the old rules of ecological coherence and of community life have remained in effect. The costs of ignoring them have accumulated, until now the boundaries of our reductive and mechanical explanations have collapsed. Their collapse reveals, plainly for all to see, the ecological and social damages that they were meant to conceal. It will seem paradoxical to some that the national and global corporate economies have narrowed the context for thinking about agriculture, but it is merely the truth. Those large economies, in their understanding and in their accounting, have excluded any concern for the land and the people. Now, in the midst of much unnecessary human and ecological damage, we are facing the necessity of a new start in agriculture.

And so it is not possible to look back at the tableau of team and tractor on that morning in 1950 and see it as I saw it then. That is not because I have changed, though obviously I have; it is because, in the fifty-four years since then, history and the law of consequence have widened the context of the scene as circles widen on water around a thrown stone.

My impatience at the slowness of the mules, I think, was a fairly representative emotion. I thought I was witnessing a contest of machine against organism, which the machine was bound to win. I did not see that the team arrived at the field that morning from the history of farming and from the farm itself, whereas the tractor arrived from almost an opposite history, and by means of a process reaching a long way beyond that farm or any farm. It took me a long time to understand that the team belonged to the farm and was directly supportable by it, whereas the tractor belonged to an economy that would remain alien to agriculture, functioning entirely by means of distant supplies and long supply lines. The tractor's arrival had signaled, among other things, agriculture's shift from an almost exclusive dependence on free solar energy to a total dependence on costly fossil fuel. But in 1950, like most people at that time, I was years away from the first inkling of the limits of the supply of cheap fuel.

We had entered an era of limitlessness, or the illusion thereof, and this in itself is a sort of wonder. My grandfather lived a life of limits, both suffered and strictly observed, in a world of limits. I learned much of that world from him and others, and then I changed; I entered the world of labor-saving machines and of limitless cheap fossil fuel. It would take me years of reading, thought, and experience to learn again that in this world limits are not only inescapable but indispensable.

My purpose here is not to disturb the question of the use of draft animals in agriculture—though I doubt that it will sleep indefinitely. I want instead to talk about the tractor as an influence. The means we use to do our work almost certainly affect the way we look at the world. If the fragment of autobiography I began with means anything, it means that my transformation from a boy who had so far grown up driving a team to a boy driving a tractor was a sight-changing experience.

Brought up as a teamster but now driving a tractor, a boy almost suddenly, almost perforce, sees the farm in a different way: as ground to be got over by a means entirely different, at an entirely different cost. The team, like the boy, would grow weary, but that weariness has all at once been subtracted, and the boy is now divided from the ground by the absence of a living connection that enforced sympathy as a practical good. The tractor can work at maximum speed hour after hour without tiring. There is no longer a reason to remember the shady spots where it was good to stop and rest. Tirelessness and speed enforce a second, more perilous change in the way the boy sees the farm: Seeing it as ground to be got over as fast as possible and, ideally, without stopping, he has taken on the psychology of a traveler by interstate highway or by air. The focus of his attention has shifted from the place to the technology.

I now suspect that if we work with machines the world will seem to us to be a machine, but if we work with living creatures the world will appear to us as a living creature. Be that as it may, mechanical farming certainly makes it easy to think mechanically about the land and its creatures. It

makes it easy to think mechanically even about oneself, and the tirelessness of tractors brought a new depth of weariness into human experience,
at a cost to health and family life that has not been fully accounted.

Once one's farm and one's thoughts have been sufficiently mechanized,
industrial agriculture's focus on production, as opposed to maintenance
or stewardship, becomes merely logical. And here the trouble completes
itself. The almost exclusive emphasis on production permits the way of
working to be determined, not by the nature and character of the farm in
its ecosystem and in its human community, but rather by the national or
the global economy and the available or affordable technology. The farm
and all concerns not immediately associated with production have in effect
disappeared from sight. The farmer too in effect has vanished. He is no
longer working as an independent and loyal agent of his place, his family,
and his community, but instead as the agent of an economy that is fundamentally adverse to him and to all that he ought to stand for.

After mechanization it is certainly possible for a farmer to maintain a
proper creaturely and stewardly awareness of the lives in her keeping. If
you look, you can still find farmers who are farming well on mechanized
farms. After mechanization, however, to maintain this kind of awareness
requires a distinct effort of will. And if we ask what are the cultural
resources that can inform and sustain such an effort of will, I believe that
we will find them gathered under the heading of *husbandry*, and here my
essay arrives finally at its subject.

-------------◆----------

The word *husbandry* is the name of a connection. In its original sense, it is
the name of the work of a domestic man, a man who has accepted a
bondage to the household. We have no cause here, I think, to raise the issue
of "sexual roles." We need only to say that our earthly life requires both
husbandry and housewifery, and that nobody, certainly no household, is
excused from a proper attendance to both.

Husbandry pertains first to the household; it connects the farm to the
household. It is an art wedded to the art of housewifery. To husband is to

use with care, to keep, to save, to make last, to conserve. Old usage tells us that there is a husbandry also of the land, of the soil, of the domestic plants and animals—obviously because of the importance of these things to the household. And there have been times, one of which is now, when some people have tried to practice a proper human husbandry of the nondomestic creatures in recognition of the dependence of our households and domestic life upon the wild world. Husbandry is the name of all the practices that sustain life by connecting us conservingly to our places and our world; it is the art of keeping tied all the strands in the living network that sustains us.

And so it appears that most and perhaps all of industrial agriculture's manifest failures are the result of an attempt to make the land produce without husbandry. The attempt to remake agriculture as a science and an industry has excluded from it the age-old husbandry that was central and essential to it, and that denoted always the fundamental domestic connections and demanded a restorative care in the use of the land and its creatures.

This effort had its initial and probably its most radical success in separating farming from the economy of subsistence. Through World War II, farm life in my region (and, I think, nearly everywhere) rested solidly upon the garden, dairy, poultry flock, and meat animals that fed the farm's family. Especially in hard times these farm families, and their farms too, survived by means of their subsistence economy. This was the husbandry and the housewifery by which the farm lived. The industrial program, on the contrary, suggested that it was "uneconomic" for a farm family to produce its own food; the effort and the land would be better applied to commercial production. The result is utterly strange in human experience: farm families who buy everything they eat at the store.

----------◆----------

An intention to replace husbandry with science was made explicit in the renaming of disciplines in the colleges of agriculture. "Soil husbandry" became "soil science," and "animal husbandry" became "animal science."

This change is worth lingering over because of what it tells us about our susceptibility to poppycock. When any discipline is made or is called a science, it is thought by some to be much increased in preciseness, complexity, and prestige. When "husbandry" becomes "science," the lowly has been exalted and the rustic has become urbane. Purporting to increase the sophistication of the humble art of farming, this change in fact brutally oversimplifies it.

"Soil science," as practiced by soil scientists, and even more as it has been handed down to farmers, has tended to treat the soil as a lifeless matrix in which "soil chemistry" takes place and "nutrients" are "made available." And this, in turn, has made farming increasingly shallow—literally so—in its understanding of the soil. The modern farm is understood as a surface on which various mechanical operations are performed, and to which various chemicals are applied. The under-surface reality of organisms and roots is mostly ignored.

"Soil husbandry" is a different kind of study, involving a different kind of mind. Soil husbandry leads, in the words of Sir Albert Howard, to understanding "health in soil, plant, animal, and man as one great subject." We apply the word "health" only to living creatures, and to soil husbandry a healthy soil is a wilderness, mostly unstudied and unknown, but teemingly alive. The soil is at once a living community of creatures and their habitat. The farm's husband, its family, its crops and animals, all are members of the soil community; all belong to the character and identity of the place. To rate the farm family merely as "labor" and its domestic plants and animals merely as "production" is thus an oversimplification, both radical and destructive.

"Science" is too simple a word to name the complex of relationships and connections that compose a healthy farm—a farm that is a full membership of the soil community. If we propose, not the reductive science we generally have, but a science of complexity, that too will be inadequate, for any complexity that science can comprehend is going to be necessarily a human construct, and therefore too simple.

The husbandry of mere humans of course cannot be complex enough either. But husbandry always has understood that what is husbanded is ultimately a mystery. A farmer, as one of his farmer correspondents once wrote to Liberty Hyde Bailey, is "a dispenser of the 'Mysteries of God.'" The mothering instinct of animals, for example, is a mystery that husbandry must use and trust mostly without understanding. The husband, unlike the "manager" or the would-be objective scientist, belongs inherently to the complexity and the mystery that is to be husbanded, and so the husband-ing mind is both careful and humble. Husbandry originates precautionary sayings like "Don't put all your eggs into one basket" and "Don't count your chickens before they hatch." It does not boast of technological feats that will "feed the world."

Husbandry, which is not replaceable by science, nevertheless uses sci-ence, and corrects it too. It is the more comprehensive discipline. To reduce husbandry to science, in practice, is to transform agricultural "wastes" into pollutants, and to subtract perennials and grazing animals from the rota-tion of crops. Without husbandry, the agriculture of science and industry has served too well the purpose of the industrial economy in reducing the number of landowners and the self-employed. It has transformed the United States from a country of many owners to a country of many employees.

--------◆--------

Without husbandry, "soil science" too easily ignores the community of creatures that live in and from, that make and are made by, the soil. Simi-larly, "animal science" without husbandry forgets, almost as a requirement, the sympathy by which we recognize ourselves as fellow creatures of the animals. It forgets that animals are so called because we once believed them to be endowed with souls. Animal science has led us away from that belief or any such belief in the sanctity of animals. It has led us instead to the ani-mal factory, which, like the concentration camp, is a vision of Hell. Animal husbandry, on the contrary, comes from and again leads to the psalmist's vision of good grass, good water, and the husbandry of God.

(It is only a little off my subject to notice also that the high and essential art of housewifery, later known as "home economics," has now become "family and consumer science." This presumably elevates the intellectual standing of the faculty by removing family life and consumption from the context—and the economy—of a home or household.)

Agriculture must mediate between nature and the human community, with ties and obligations in both directions. To farm well requires an elaborate courtesy toward all creatures, animate and inanimate. It is sympathy that most appropriately enlarges the context of human work. Contexts become wrong by being too small—too small, that is, to contain the scientist or the farmer or the farm family or the local ecosystem or the local community—and this is crucial. "Out of context," as Wes Jackson has said, "the best minds do the worst damage."

Looking for a way to give an exact sense of this necessary sympathy, the *feeling* of husbandry at work, I found it in a book entitled *Feed My Sheep* by Terry Cummins. Mr. Cummins is a man of about my age, who grew up farming with his grandfather in Pendleton County, Kentucky, in the 1940s and early 50s. In the following sentences he is remembering himself at the age of thirteen, in about 1947:

> When you see that you're making the other things feel good, it gives you a good feeling, too.
>
> The feeling inside sort of just happens, and you can't say this did it or that did it. It's the many little things. It doesn't seem that taking sweat-soaked harnesses off tired, hot horses would be something that would make you notice. Opening a barn door for the sheep standing out in a cold rain, or throwing a few grains of corn to the chickens are small things, but these little things begin to add up in you, and you can begin to understand that you're important. You may not be real important like people who do great things that you read about in the newspaper, but you begin to feel that you're important to all the life around you. Nobody else knows or cares too much about what you do, but if you get a good feeling inside about what you do, then it doesn't matter if nobody else knows. I do think about myself a lot when

I'm alone way back on the place bringing in the cows or sitting on a mowing machine all day. But when I start thinking about how our animals and crops and fields and woods and gardens sort of all fit together, then I get that good feeling inside and don't worry much about what will happen to me.

This passage goes to the heart of what I am trying to say, because it goes to the heart of farming as I have known it. Mr. Cummins's sentences describe an experience regrettably and perhaps dangerously missing now from the childhood of most children. They also describe the communion between the farmer as husband and the well-husbanded farm. This communion is a cultural force that can exist only by becoming personal. To see it so described is to understand at once how necessary and how threatened it now is.

I have tried to say what husbandry is, how it works, and why it is necessary. Now I want to speak of two paramount accomplishments of husbandry to which I think we will have to pay more deliberate attention, in our present circumstances, than we ever have before. These are local adaptation and local coherence of form. It is strange that a science of agriculture founded on evolutionary biology, with its practical emphasis on survival, would exempt the human species from these concerns.

True husbandry, as its first strategy of survival, has always striven to fit the farming to the farm and to the field, to the needs and abilities of the farm's family, and to the local economy. Every wild creature is the product of such an adaptive process. The same process once was a dominant influence on agriculture, for the cost of ignoring it was hunger. One striking and well-known example of local adaptation in agriculture is the number and diversity of British sheep breeds, most of which are named for the localities in which they were developed. But local adaptation must be even more refined than this example suggests, for it involves consideration of the individuality of every farm and every field.

Our recent focus upon productivity, genetic and technological uniformity, and global trade—all supported by supposedly limitless supplies of fuel, water, and soil—has obscured the necessity for local adaptation. But our circumstances are changing rapidly now, and this requirement will be forced upon us again by terrorism and other kinds of political violence, by chemical pollution, by increasing energy costs, by depleted soils, aquifers, and streams, and by the spread of exotic weeds, pests, and diseases. We are going to have to return to the old questions about local nature, local carrying capacities, and local needs. And we are going to have to resume the breeding of plants and animals to fit the region and the farm.

The same obsessions and extravagances that have caused us to ignore the issue of local adaptation have at the same time caused us to ignore the issue of form. These two issues are so closely related that it is difficult to talk about one without talking about the other. During the half century and more of our neglect of local adaptation, we have subjected our farms to a radical oversimplification of form. The diversified and reasonably self-sufficient farms of my region and of many other regions have been conglomerated into larger farms with larger fields, increasingly specialized, and subjected increasingly to the strict, unnatural linearity of the production line.

But the first requirement of a form is that it must be comprehensive; it must not leave out something that essentially belongs within it. The farm that Terry Cummins remembers was remarkably comprehensive, and it was not any one of its several enterprises alone that made him feel good, but rather "how our animals and crops and fields and woods and gardens sort of all fit together."

The form of the farm must answer to the farmer's feeling for the place, its creatures, and its work. It is a never-ending effort of fitting together many diverse things. It must incorporate the life cycle and the fertility cycles of animals. It must bring crops and livestock into balance and mutual support. It must be a pattern on the ground and in the mind. It must be at once ecological, agricultural, economic, familial, and neighborly. It must be inclusive enough, complex enough, coherent, intelligible, and durable. It must have within its limits the completeness of an organism or an ecosystem, or of any other good work of art.

The making of a form begins in the recognition and acceptance of limits. The farm is limited by its topography, its climate, its ecosystem, its human neighborhood and local economy, and of course by the larger economies, and by the preferences and abilities of the farmer. The true husbandman shapes the farm within an assured sense of what it cannot be and what it should not be. And thus the problem of form returns us to that of local adaptation.

The task before us, now as always before, is to renew and husband the means, both natural and human, of agriculture. But to talk now about renewing husbandry is to talk about unsimplifying what is in reality an extremely complex subject. This will require us to accept again, and more competently than before, the health of the ecosystem, the farm, and the human community as the ultimate standard of agricultural performance.

Unsimplification is difficult, I imagine, in any circumstances; our present circumstances will make it especially so. Soon the majority of the world's people will be living in cities. We are now obliged to think of so many people demanding the means of life from the land, to which they will no longer have a practical connection, and of which they will have little knowledge. We are obliged also to think of the consequences of any attempt to meet this demand by large-scale, expensive, petroleum-dependent technological schemes that will ignore local conditions and local needs. The problem of renewing husbandry, and the need to promote a general awareness of everybody's agricultural responsibilities, thus becomes urgent.

How are we to do this? How can we restore a competent husbandry to the minds of the world's producers and consumers?

For a start of course we must recognize that this effort is already in progress on many farms and in many urban consumer groups scattered across our country and the world. But we must recognize too that this effort needs an authorizing focus and force that would grant it a new legitimacy, intellectual rigor, scientific respectability, and responsible teaching. There are many reasons to hope that this might be supplied by our colleges of agriculture, and there are some reasons to think that this hope is not fantastical.

With that hope in mind, I want to return to the precaution that I mentioned earlier. The effort of husbandry is partly scientific, but it is entirely cultural, and a cultural initiative can exist only by becoming personal. It will become increasingly clear, I believe, that agricultural scientists, and the rest of us as well, are going to have to be less specialized, or less isolated by our specialization. Agricultural scientists will need to work as indwelling members of agricultural communities or of consumer communities. Their scientific work will need to accept the limits and the influence of that membership. It is not irrational to propose that a significant number of these scientists should be farmers, and so subject their scientific work, and that of their colleagues, to the influence of a farmer's practical circumstances. Along with the rest of us, they will need to accept all the imperatives of husbandry as the context of their work. We cannot keep things from falling apart in our society if they do not cohere in our minds and in our lives.

(2004)

Agriculture from the Roots Up*

HENRY DAVID THOREAU wrote somewhere that hundreds are hacking at the branches for every one who is striking at the root. He meant this as a metaphor, but it applies literally to modern agriculture and to the science of modern agriculture. As it has become more and more industrialized, agriculture increasingly has been understood as an enterprise established upon the surface of the ground. Most people nowadays lack even a superficial knowledge of agriculture, and most who do know something about it are paying little or no attention to what is happening under the surface.

The scientists at The Land Institute in Salina, Kansas, on the contrary, are striking at the root. Their study of the root and the roots of our agricultural problems has produced a radical criticism, leading to a proposed solution that is radical.

Their criticism is made radical by one crucial choice: the adoption of the natural ecosystem as the *first* standard of agricultural performance, having priority over the standard of productivity and certainly over the delusional and dangerous industrial standard of "efficiency." That single change makes a momentous difference, one that is historical and cultural as well as scientific.

By the standard of the natural or the healthy ecosystem, we see as if suddenly the shortcomings, not only of industrial agriculture but of agriculture itself, insofar as agriculture has consisted of annual monocultures. To

*Written originally as a speech for a Land Institute symposium, "Perennial Solutions to the Annual Problem," Seattle, November 3, 2004.

those of us who are devoted to agriculture in any of its historical forms, such criticism is inevitably painful. And yet we may see its justice and accept it, understanding how much is at stake. To others, who have founded their careers or their businesses precisely upon the shortcomings of agriculture as we now have it, this criticism will perhaps be even more painful, and no doubt they will resist with all the great power we know they have.

Even so, this is a criticism for which the time is ripe. A rational denial of its justice is no longer possible. There are many reasons for this, but the main one, I think, is the virtual meltdown of the old boundaries of specialist thought in agriculture—a meltdown that I hope foretells the same fate for the boundaries of all specialist thought.

The justifying assumptions of the industrial agriculture that we now have are based on a reductive science working within strictly bounded specializations. This agriculture, an agglomeration of specialties, appeared perfectly rational and salutary so long as it was assumable that efficiency and productivity were adequate standards, that husbandry was safely reducible to science and fertility to chemistry, that organisms are merely machines, that agriculture is under no obligation to nature, that it has only agricultural results, and that it can be confidently based upon "cheap" fossil fuels.

The inventors of this agriculture assumed, in short, that the human will is sovereign in the universe, that the only laws are the laws of mechanics, and that the material world and its "natural resources" are without limit. These are the assumptions that, acknowledged or not, underlie the "war" by which we humans have undertaken to "conquer" nature, and which is the dominant myth of modern intellectual life.

----------◆----------

In the days of human darkness and ignorance, now supposedly past, we found ways to acknowledge the sanctity of nature and to honor her as the common mother of all creatures, including ourselves. We conducted our relations with her by prayer, propitiation, skilled work, thrift, caution, and care. Our concern about that relationship produced the concepts of

usufruct and stewardship. A few lines from the "Two Cantos of Mutabili-
tie" that Edmund Spenser placed at the end of *The Faerie Queene* will suffice
to give a sense of our ancient veneration:

> Then forth issewed (great goddesse) great dame Nature,
> With goodly port and gracious Majesty;
> Being far greater and more tall of stature
> Than any of the gods or Powers on hie . . .
>
> .   .   .   .
>
> This great Grandmother of all creatures bred
> Great Nature, ever young yet full of eld,
> Still moving, yet unmoved from her sted;
> Unseen of any, yet of all beheld . . .

Thus, though he was a Christian, Spenser still saw fit at the end of the sixteenth century to present Nature as the genius of the sublunary world, a
figure of the greatest majesty, mystery, and power, the source of all earthly
life. He addressed her, in addition, as the supreme judge of all her creatures,
ruling by standards that we would now call ecological:

> Who Right to all dost deal indifferently,
> Damning all Wrong and tortious Injurie,
> Which any of thy creatures do to other
> (Oppressing them with power, unequally)
> Sith of them all thou art the equall mother,
> And knittest each to each, as brother unto brother.

And then, at about Spenser's time or a little after, we set forth in our "war
against nature" with the purpose of conquering her and wringing her powerful and lucrative secrets from her by various forms of "tortious Injurie."
This we have thought of as our "enlightenment" and as "progress." But in
the event this war, like most wars, has turned out to be a trickier business
than we expected. We must now face two shocking surprises. The first surprise is that if we say and believe that we are at war with nature, then we are

in the fullest sense at war: that is, we are both opposing and being opposed, and the costs to both sides are extremely high.

The second surprise is that we are not winning. On the evidence now available, we have to conclude that we are losing—and, moreover, that there was never a chance that we could win. Despite the immense power and violence that we have deployed against her, nature is handing us one defeat after another. Even in our most grievous offenses against her—as in the present epidemic of habitat destruction and species extinction—we are being defeated, for in the long run we can less afford the losses than nature can. And we have to look upon soil erosion and the spread of exotic diseases, weeds, and pests as nature's direct reprisals for our violations of her laws. Sometimes she seems terrifyingly serene in her triumphs over us, as when, simply by refusing to absorb our pollutants, she forces us to live in our mess.

Thus she has forced us to recognize that the context of American agriculture is not merely fields and farms or the free market or the economy, but it is also the polluted Mississippi River, the hypoxic zone in the Gulf of Mexico, all the small towns whose drinking water contains pesticides and nitrates, the pumped-down aquifers and the no-longer-flowing rivers, and all the lands that we have scalped, gouged, poisoned, or destroyed utterly for "cheap" fuels and raw materials.

Thus she is forcing us to believe what the great teachers and prophets have always told us and what the ecologists are telling us again: All things are connected; the context of everything is everything else. By now, many of us know, and more are learning, that if you want to evaluate the agriculture of a region, you must begin, not with a balance sheet, but with the local water. How continuously do the small streams flow? How clear is the water? How much sediment and how many pollutants are carried in the runoff? Are the ponds and creeks and rivers fit for swimming? Can you eat the fish?

We know, or we are learning, that from the questions about water we go naturally to questions about the soil. Is it staying in place? What is its water-holding capacity? Does it drain well? How much humus is in it?

What of its biological health? How often and for how long is it exposed to the weather? How deep in it do the roots go?

———————◆———————

Such are the questions that trouble and urge and inspire the scientists at The Land Institute, for everything depends upon the answers. The answers, as these scientists know, will reveal not only the state of the health of the landscape, but also the state of the culture of the people who inhabit and use the landscape. Is it a culture of respect, thrift, and seemly skills, or a culture of indifference and mechanical force? A culture of life, or a culture of death?

And beyond those questions are questions insistently practical and economic, questions of accounting. What is the worth, to us humans with our now insupportable health care industry, of ecological health? Is our health in any way separable from the health of our economic landscapes? Must not the health of water and soil be accounted an economic asset? Will not this greater health support, sustain, and in the long run cheapen the productivity of our farms?

If our war against nature destroys the health of water and soil, and thus inevitably the health of agriculture and our own health, and can only lead to our economic ruin, then we need to try another possibility. And there is only one: If we cannot establish an enduring or even a humanly bearable economy by our attempt to defeat nature, then we will have to try living in harmony and cooperation with her.

By its adoption of the healthy ecosystem as the appropriate standard of agricultural performance, The Land Institute has rejected competition as the fundamental principle of economics, and therefore of the applied sciences, and has replaced it with the principle of harmony. In doing so, it has placed its work within a lineage and tradition that predates both industrialism and modern science. The theme of a human and even an economic harmony with nature goes back many hundreds of years in the literary record. Its age in the prehistoric cultures can only be conjectured, but we may confidently assume that it is ancient, probably as old as the human race. In the early twentieth century this theme was applied explicitly to agriculture by writers such as F. H. King, Liberty Hyde Bailey, J. Russell Smith, Sir Albert Howard, and Aldo Leopold, Howard being the one who gave it the soundest and most elaborate scientific underpinning. This modern lineage was interrupted by the juggernaut of industrial agriculture following World War II. But in the 1970s, when Wes Jackson began thinking about the Kansas prairie as a standard and model for Kansas farming, he took up the old theme at about where Howard had left it, doing so remarkably without previous knowledge of Howard.

And so, in espousing the principle and the goal of harmony, The Land Institute acquired an old and honorable ancestry. It acquired at the same time, in the same way, a working principle also old and honorable: that of art as imitation of nature. The initiating question was this: If, so to speak, you place a Kansas wheatfield beside a surviving patch of the native Kansas prairie, what is the difference?

Well, the primary difference, obvious to any observer, is that, whereas the wheatfield is a monoculture of annuals, the plant community of the prairie is highly diverse and perennial. There are many implications in that difference, not all of which are agricultural, but five of which are of immediate and urgent agricultural interest: The prairie's loss of soil to erosion is minimal; it is highly efficient in its ability to absorb, store, and use water; it makes the maximum use of every year's sunlight; it builds and preserves its own fertility; and it protects itself against pests and diseases.

The next question, the practical one, follows logically and naturally from the first: How might we contrive, let us say, a Kansas farm in imitation of a Kansas prairie, acquiring for agriculture the several ecological services of the prairie along with the economic benefit of a sufficient harvest of edible seeds? And so we come to the great project of The Land Institute.

I lack the technical proficiency to comment at much length on this work. I would like to end simply by saying how I believe the science now in practice at The Land Institute differs from the science of industrial agriculture.

---◆---

We are living in an age of technological innovation. Our preoccupation with invention and novelty has begun, by this late day, to look rather absurd, especially in our strict avoidance of cost accounting. What invention, after all, has done more net good or given more net pleasure than soap? And who invented soap? It is all too easy, under the circumstances, to imagine a media publicist snatching at The Land Institute's project as "innovation on an epic scale" or "the next revolution in agriculture" or "the new scientific frontier."

But these scientists are contemplating no such thing. Their vision and their work does not arise from or lead to any mechanical or chemical breakthrough; it does not depend on any newly discovered fuel. The innovation they have in mind is something old under the sun: a better adaptation of the human organism to its natural habitat. They are not seeking to implement a technological revolution or a revolution of any kind. They are interested merely in improving our fundamental relationship to the earth, changing the kind of roots we put down and deepening the depth we put them down to. This is not revolutionary, because it is merely a part of a long job that we have not finished, that we have tried for a little while to finish in the wrong way, but one that we will never finish if we do it the right way. Harmony between our human economy and the natural world—local adaptation—is a perfection we will never finally achieve but must continuously try for. There is never a finality to it because it involves living creatures who change. The soil has living creatures in it. It has live roots in it, perennial roots if it is lucky. If it is the soil of the right kind of farm, it has a farm family growing out of it. The work of adaptation must go on because the world changes; our places change and we change; we change our places and our places change us. The science of adaptation, then, is unending. Anybody who undertakes to adapt agriculture to a place—or, in J. Russell Smith's words, to fit the farming to the farm—will never run out of problems or want for intellectual stimulation.

The science of The Land Institute promptly exposes the weakness of the annual thought of agricultural industrialism because it measures its work by the standard of the natural ecosystem, which gives pride of place to perennials. It exposes also the weakness of the top-down thought of technological innovation by proceeding from the roots up, and by aiming, not at universality and uniformity, but at local adaptation. It would deepen the formal limits of agricultural practice many feet below the roots of the annual grain crops, but it would draw in the limits of concern to the local watershed, ecosystem, farm, and field. This is by definition a science of place, operating within a world of acknowledged limits—of space, time, energy, soil, water, and human intelligence. It is a science facing, in the most local and intimate terms, a world of daunting formal complexity and of an ultimately impenetrable mystery—exactly the world that the reductive sciences of industrial agriculture have sought to oversimplify and thus ignore. This new science, in its ancient quest, demands the acceptance of human ignorance as the ever-present starting point of human work, and it requires the use of all the intelligence we have.

(2004)

Local Knowledge in the Age of Information*

IN 1983, REVIEWING A BOOK of agricultural essays by Wes Jackson and one by me, Lewis Hyde suggested that our two books were part of an effort of the periphery to be heard by the center. This has stayed in my mind as perhaps the most useful thing that has been said about my agricultural writing and that of my allies. It is useful because the dichotomy between center and periphery does in fact exist, as does the tendency of the center to be ignorant of the periphery.

These terms appear to be plain enough, but as I am going to use them here they may need a little clarification. We can say, for example, that a land grant university is a center with a designated periphery which it is supposed to maintain and improve. Or an industrial city is a center with a periphery which it is bound to influence and which, according to its politics and its power, it may either conserve or damage. Or a national or a state government is a center solemnly entrusted with responsibility for peripheral places, but in general it extends its protections and favors to the commercial centers, which outvote or out-"contribute" the periphery. But above all, now, as a sort of center of centers, is the global "free market" economy of the great corporations, the periphery of which is everywhere, and for its periphery this center expresses no concern and acknowledges no responsibility.

---

*Written originally as a speech for the conference, "Globalization of Information: Agriculture at the Crossroads," at the University of Kentucky; delivered on May 17, 2005.

The global economy is a development—it is intended apparently as the culmination—of the technological and commercial colonialist orthodoxy that has dominated the world increasingly since the Renaissance, the principle of the orthodoxy being that any commercial entity is entitled to wealth according to its power. A center, then, as I will use the term, is wherever the wealth, power, and knowledge of this overbearing economy have accumulated. Modern technology, as it has developed from oceanic navigation to the World Wide Web, has been increasingly a centralizing force, enabling ever larger accumulations of wealth, power, and knowledge in an ever smaller number of centers.

Since my concern here is with the need for communication—or, as I would prefer to say, conversation—between periphery and center, I must begin with the center's characteristic ignorance of the periphery. This, I suppose, must always have been so, even of the market towns of the world before the Renaissance. But in that older world, the cities and towns mostly (though with significant exceptions) could take for granted that their tributary landscapes were populated by established rural communities that knew both how to make the land produce and how to take care of it.

It is still true that the center is supported by the periphery. All human economy is still land-based. To the extent that we must eat and drink and be clothed, sheltered, and warmed, we live from the land. The idea that we have now progressed from a land-based economy to an economy based on information is a fantasy.

It is still true also that the people of the center believe that the people of the periphery will always supply their needs from the land and will always keep the land productive: There will always be an abundance of food, fiber, timber, and fuel. This too is a fantasy. It is not known, but is simply taken for granted.

As its power of attraction increases, the center becomes more ignorant of the periphery. And under the pervasive influence of the center, the economic landscapes of the periphery have fewer and fewer inhabitants who know them well and know how to care properly for them. Many rural areas are now populated mostly by urban people.

In the *New York Review of Books* of March 24, 2005, Clifford Geertz wrote that tsunamis and other large-scale disasters threaten "the conviction that perhaps most reconciles many of us . . . to our own mortality: that, though we ourselves may perish, the community into which we were born, and the sort of life it supports, will somehow live on." But except for a few of the better-established Amish communities, this conviction is an illusion; one cannot imagine how Mr. Geertz has held onto it. No matter even if "we" have stayed put geographically, if we are over thirty, or maybe even twenty, the community in which we live is by now radically unlike "the community in which we were born." In fact, there are now many people whose native communities have not only been radically changed but have been completely destroyed by some form of "development." Since the end of World War II, the economic, technological, and social forces of industrialism have pretty thoroughly disintegrated the rural communities of the United States and, I believe, of other parts of the world also, inducing in them a "mobility" that has boiled over in the cities, disintegrating them as well.

The loss of the old life of the rural communities has usually been written off as an improvement, and only sometimes lamented. Nowhere that I know has it been more knowingly and poignantly lamented than in Ernest J. Gaines's novel, *A Gathering of Old Men*, set on a sugarcane plantation in Louisiana. Here the man named Johnny Paul is speaking for the community of black field hands that he knew as a growing boy:

> Thirty, forty of us going out in the field with cane knives, hoes, plows—name it. Sunup to sundown, hard, miserable work, but we managed to get it done. We stuck together, shared what little we had, and loved and respected each other.
>
> But just look at things today. Where the people? Where the roses? Where the four-o'clocks? The palm-of-Christians? Where the people used to sing and pray in the church? I'll tell you. Under them trees back there, that's where. And where they

used to stay, the weeds got it now, just waiting for the tractor to come plow it up.

. . . .

You had to be here then to be able to don't see it . . . now. But I was here then, and I don't see it now . . . I was scared . . . one day that tractor was go'n come in there and plow up them graves, getting rid of all proof that we ever was. Like now they trying to get rid of all proof that black people ever farmed this land with plows and mules—like if they had nothing from the starten but motor machines . . . . Mama and Papa worked too hard in these fields. They mama and they papa worked too hard in these same fields. They mama and they papa people worked too hard, too hard to have that tractor just come in that graveyard and destroy all proof that they ever was. I'm the last one left.

This too is part of an effort of the periphery to be heard by the center.

Johnny Paul's speech, of which I have quoted only a part, is obviously eloquent and as deeply moving as he is deeply moved, but still we are left with the question: Was what he was lamenting actually lamentable? To begin to answer that question, we have to answer another: Was what those people knew about their place of any value to their place and to people in other places? Or, to state the question a little more thematically, is there a practical reason for the periphery to be heard by the center?

————◆————

Insofar as the center is utterly dependent upon the periphery, its ignorance of the periphery is not natural or necessary, but is merely dangerous. The danger is increased when this ignorance protects itself by contempt for the people who know. If the most intimate knowledge of the land from which you live belongs to people whom you consider to be provincials or field niggers or hillbillies or hicks or rednecks, then you are not likely ever to learn very much.

Furthermore, the danger increases as the periphery is enlarged; the vulnerability of long supply lines is well understood. To give the most obvious example, the United States has chosen (if that is the right word) to become an import-dependent society rather than to live principally from its own land and the work of its own people, as if dependence on imported goods and labor can be consistent with political independence and self-determination. This inconsistency is making us, willy-nilly, an imperial power, which perhaps increases "business opportunities" for our government's corporate sponsors, but certainly increases our fragility and our peril. The economic independence of families, communities, and even regions has now been almost completely destroyed.

Far from caring for our land and our rural people, as we would do if we understood our dependence on them, we have not, as a nation, given them so much as a serious thought for half a century. I read, I believe, my full share of commentary on politics and economics by accredited experts, and I can assure you that you will rarely find in any of them even a passing reference to agriculture or forestry. Our great politicians seem only dimly aware that an actual *country* lies out there beyond the places of power, wealth, and knowledge. The ultimate official word on agriculture seems to have been spoken by Dwight Eisenhower's secretary of agriculture, Ezra Taft Benson, who told the farmers to "Get big or get out."

A predominantly urban population that is contemptuous of the working people of the farms and forests cannot know enough about the country to exercise a proper responsibility for its good use. And ignorance in the center promotes ignorance on the periphery. Knowledge that is not properly valued decreases in value, and so finally is lost. It is not possible to uproot virtually the whole agricultural population by economic adversity, replacing it with machines and chemicals, and still keep local knowledge of the land and land use at a high level of competence. We still know how to make the land produce, but only temporarily, for we are losing the knowledge of how to keep it productive. Wes Jackson has written and often said that when the ratio of eyes to acres in agricultural landscapes becomes too wide, when the number of caretakers declines below a level that varies from place to place but is reckonable for every place, then good husbandry of the land becomes impossible.

The general complacency about such matters seems to rest on the assumption that science can serve as a secure connection between land and people, designing beneficent means and methods of land use and assuring the quality and purity of our food. But we cannot escape or ignore the evidence that this assumption is false.

There is, to begin with, too great a gap between the science and the practice of agriculture. This gap is inherent in the present organization of intellectual and academic life, and it formalizes the differences between knowing and doing, the laboratory or classroom and the world. It is generally true that agricultural scientists are consumers rather than producers of agricultural products. They eat with the same freedom from farmwork, weather, and the farm economy as other consumers, and perhaps with the same naïve confidence that a demand will dependably call forth a supply.

Moreover, the official agriculture of science, government, and agribusiness has been concerned almost exclusively with the ability of the land to produce food and fiber, and ultimately salaries, grants, and profits. It has correspondingly neglected its ecological and social responsibilities, and also, in many ways, its agricultural ones. It has ignored agriculture's continuing obligations to be diverse, conservative of its means, and respectful of its natural supports.

The assumption that science can serve as an adequate connector between people and land, and thus can effectively replace the common knowledge and culture of local farm communities, by now has the status of an official program—though the aim of science, more often than not, is to connect capital with profit. The ascendancy of the expert involves a withdrawal or relinquishment of confidence in local intelligence—that is, in the knowledge, experience, and mental competence of ordinary people doing ordinary work. The result, naturally, is that the competence of local intelligence has declined. We are losing the use of local minds at work on local problems. The right way to deal with a problem, supposedly, is to summon an expert from government, industry, or a university, who will recommend the newest centrally-devised mechanical or chemical solution. Thus capital supposedly replaces intelligence as the basis of work, just as information supposedly replaces land as the basis of the economy.

This would be fine, of course, if the recommended solutions were in fact solving the problems. But too often they not only fail to solve the problems, but either make them worse or replace them with new problems. And so, as we continue our enterprise of "sound science" and technological progress, our agriculture becomes more and more toxic, specialized, and impoverished of genes, breeds, and varieties; we deplete the aquifers and the rivers; our rural communities die; our fields and our food become less healthful; our food supply becomes ever more dependent on long-distance transportation and immigrant labor; our water becomes less drinkable; the hypoxic zone grows in the Gulf of Mexico.

These calamities of industrial agriculture define our need to take seriously Wes Jackson's insistence that we need a farm population large, alert, and skilled enough, not just to make the land produce, but to take the best possible care of it as well. At present we are so far from this goal that a number of depopulated rural communities in the prairie states are offering free land and other economic incentives to new settlers.

But we need to consider the possibility that even our remnant farm population possesses knowledge and experience that is indispensable in a rapidly urbanizing world. The center may need to pay attention to the periphery and accept its influence simply in order to survive. I have at hand three testimonials to the value of peripheral knowledge, and remarkably they all come from scientists. The first is from Robert B. Weeden, a biologist and writer who has done much of his work in Alaska:

> If science took on a regional/local focus, one result would be that, for the first time in three centuries, the gap between scientist and citizen would start to close.... [W]hat we would see is that the conduct of critiqued experiment (science) and the close

observation of unfolding life (common sense) would form a team. I watched this notion be born and begin its childhood in Alaska's north. Scientists, newcomers from the south, were hired by federal agencies and oil corporations to find out something about the environments in which petroleum exploration and production would occur. Time was scarcer than money. Some of the scientists had enough casual conversation with Inuit and Yupik people to realize that if you wanted guides to the seasonal behavior of sea ice and its inhabitants, local people were far better sources than the thin and inadequate records of earlier scientists. The informal conversation grew into formal conferences, funding, and ongoing committees. To be honest, government and corporate motives were mixed, because, in addition to knowing something, native people also controlled access to places the oil folk wanted to explore. Nevertheless, two systems of knowledge did come together.

My second witness is the geographer, Carl Sauer, who wrote:

If I should move to the center of the mass I should feel that the germinal potential was out there on the periphery.

And, finally, I offer a rather emphatic statement form the biologist Roger Payne's book, *Among Whales*:

[A]ny observant local knows more than any visiting scientist. Always. No exceptions.

———◆———

That the center at present is ignorantly dependent on the periphery does not suggest that the center is somehow inherently worthless. It is not. The periphery needs a center, just as a center needs a periphery. One is unthinkable without the other. The center collects and stores things of value. It is a place of economic and cultural exchange. It is the right place for a stockyard or a university. The distinction I am working toward is that between an ignorant center and one that is properly knowledgeable, and also that between an ignorant periphery and one that is properly knowledgeable. The critical point is that to be properly knowledgeable each must be in conversation with the other. They must know the truth of their interdependence; they must know what they *owe* to each other.

To speak of a need for knowledge, I know, is to put oneself in danger of being run over by the information economy and the communications industry hastening to the rescue with computers, data banks, PA systems, photocopiers, leaflets, and Power Point presentations. Despite my reputation as a Luddite, I don't want to say that the information economy is useless, but I would like to say several things meant to burden it and slow it down, and (let us hope) improve it.

First, let us consider how we have degraded this word *information*. As you would expect, in-form-ation in its root meaning has to do with the idea of form: a pattern, structure, or ordering principle. To in-form is to form from within. *Information*, in this sense, refers to teaching and learning, to the formation of a person's mind or character. But we seem to be using the word now almost exclusively to refer to a random accumulation of facts, all having the one common characteristic of availability; they can, as we are too likely to say, be "accessed." Sometimes they are available at little cost—from a public library, say, or an Extension Service bulletin. Sometimes they are available only as "intellectual property," which is available at the seller's price. At whatever cost this information is made available to its potential users, it arrives unformed and unexperienced. There is nothing deader or of more questionable value than facts in isolation.

And this exposes the problem of an information economy. The problem is in determining the value of the commodity, information being much harder to evaluate than real goods such as food, clothing, and shelter. The value of information is in its usefulness in manipulating, for better or worse, the natural world. If the result is "for better," then the information can be accounted an asset; if "for worse," then it must be booked as a liability, of less than no value. But until the information is shaped into knowledge in some particular mind and applied with or without harm to an actual place, we will not know whether or not it is an asset or how valuable an asset it is.

This warehousing of accessible information is obviously an activity of the center. Information of this sort is one of the commodities that the center collects and dispenses to the periphery. The center, as we now say, "communicates" with the periphery, the market or the factory or the university communicates with the countryside, by means of this information. Sometimes the information is sent out encoded in various kinds of technology, sometimes in printed instructions or reports, sometimes in radio or television broadcasts. And this communication is a connection between the center and the periphery.

------------◆------------

But let us consider, secondly, that this is only half a connection. It is a one-way communication between an active sender and a passive receiver. This is why I said earlier that I prefer conversation to communication. Communication, as we have learned from our experience with the media, goes one way, from the center outward to the periphery. But a conversation goes two ways; in a conversation the communication goes back and forth. A conversation, unlike a "communication," cannot be prepared ahead of time, and it is changed as it goes along by what is said. Nobody beginning a conversation can know how it will end. And there is always the possibility that a conversation, by bringing its participants under one another's influence, will change them, possibly for the better. (*Conversation*, as I understand the term, refers to talk between or among people for their mutual edification. This excludes talk shows or call-in programs, which are commodities for consumption by a nonparticipating audience.)

Once we have proposed a conversation between center and periphery, we see immediately that what the periphery has to say to the center is critically different from what the center has to say, or at least from what it presently is saying, to the periphery.

The information that is accumulated at the center—at the corporate or academic or governmental end of the information economy—and then dispersed to the periphery tends necessarily toward the abstract or universal, toward general applicability. The Holstein cow and the Roundup-ready soybean are, in this sense, abstractions: the artifacts of a centrally divised agriculture, in use everywhere without respect to place or to any need for local adaptation. When the periphery accepts these things uncritically, adopting the ideas and the language of the center, then it has begun to belong to the center, and usually at a considerable long-term cost to itself. The immediate cost is the loss of knowledge and language specific to localities.

But the question we are trying to raise here is: How can the best work be done? Or: How can we give the best possible care to our highly variable economic landscapes, in which no two woodlands, no two farms, and no two fields are exactly alike? If we are ever to get the right answers to this question, then the people of the periphery will have to cultivate and cherish knowledge of their places and communities, which are always to some extent unique. This will be *placed* knowledge; out of place, it is little better than ignorance; and it is learnable only at home. To speak of it will require a *placed* language, made in reference to local names, conditions, and needs. Moreover, the people of the center need to know that this local knowledge is a necessary knowledge of *their* world. They need to hear the local languages with understanding and respect—no more talk about "hicks" and "provincials" and "rednecks." A refined, discriminating knowledge of localities by the local people is indispensable if we want the most sensitive application of intelligence to local problems, if we want the best work to be done, if we want the world to last. If we give up the old orientation of agriculture to the nature of individual farms and fields, and reorient it to industry, industrial technology, and the global economy, then the result is uniformity, oversimplification, overspecialization, and (inevitably) destruction.

To use the handiest practical example, I am talking about the need for a two-way communication, a conversation, between a land grant university and the region for and to which it is responsible. The idea of the extension service should be applied to the whole institution. Not just the agricultural extension agents, but also the graduate teachers, doctors, lawyers, and other community servants should be involved. They should be carrying news from the university out into its region, of course. But this would be extension in two directions: They would also be carrying back into the university news of what is happening that works well, what is succeeding according to the best standards, what works locally. And they should be carrying back criticism also: what is *not* working, what the university is not doing that it should do, what it is doing that it should do better.

Communication is not necessarily cooperative. "Get big or get out" is a communication, and hardly expectant of a reply. But conversation is necessarily cooperative, and it can carry us, far beyond the principle of competition, to an understanding of common interest. By conversation a university or a city and its region could define themselves as one community rather than an assortment of competing interests. Center and periphery, city and country, consumers and producers do not have to define themselves as economic adversaries. They can begin to be a community simply by asking: What can we do for each other? What do you need that we can supply you with or do for you? What do you need to know that we can tell you?

Once the conversation has started, it will quickly become obvious, I think, that there must be a common, agreed-upon standard of judgment; and I think this will have to be health: the health of ecosystems and of human communities.

There will have to be also a common idea, or hope, of economic justice. The operative principles here would be production controls, to prevent surpluses from being used as a weapon against producers; and fairness, granting to small producers and tradespeople the same marketing advantages as to large ones. And so good-bye to volume discounts.

--------◆--------

My third point is that the means of human communication are limited, and that we dare not forget this. There is some knowledge that cannot be communicated by communication technology, the accumulation of tape-recorded "oral histories" not withstanding. For what may be the most essential knowledge, how to work well in one's place, language simply is not an adequate vehicle. To return again to land use as an example, farming itself, like life itself, is different from information or knowledge or anything else that can be verbally communicated. It is not just the local application of science; it is also the local practice of a local art and the living of a local life.

As farmers never tire of repeating, you can't learn to farm by reading a book, and you can't *tell* somebody how to farm. Older farmers I knew used to be fond of saying, "I can't tell you how to do that, but I can put you where you can learn." There is such a thing, then, as incommunicable knowledge, knowledge that comes only by experience and by association.

There is in addition for us humans, always, the unknown, things perhaps that we need to know that we do not know and are never going to know. There is mystery. Obvious as it is, we easily forget that beyond our sciences and our arts, beyond our technology and our language, is the irreducible reality of our precious world that somehow, so far, has withstood our demands and accommodated our life, and of which we will always be dangerously ignorant.

Our great modern powers of science, technology, and industry are always offering themselves to us with the suggestion that we know enough to use them well, that we are intelligent enough to act without limit in our own behalf. But the evidence is now rapidly mounting against us. By living as we do, in our ignorance and our pride, we are diminishing our world and the possibility of life.

This is a plea for humility.

(2005)

The Burden of the Gospels*

ANYBODY HALF AWAKE these days will be aware that there are many Christians who are exceedingly confident in their understanding of the Gospels, and who are exceedingly self-confident in their understanding of themselves in their faith. They appear to know precisely the purposes of God, and they appear to be perfectly assured that they are now doing, and in every circumstance will continue to do, precisely God's will as it applies specifically to themselves. They are confident, moreover, that God hates people whose faith differs from their own, and they are happy to concur in that hatred.

Having been invited to speak to a convocation of Christian seminarians, I at first felt that I should say nothing until I confessed that I do not have any such confidence. And then I understood that this would have to be my subject. I would have to speak of the meaning, as I understand it, of my lack of confidence, which I think is not at all the same as a lack of faith.

It is a fact that I have spent my life, for the most part willingly, under the influence of the Bible, particularly the Gospels, and of the Christian tradition in literature and the other arts. As a child, sometimes unwillingly, I learned many of the Bible's stories and teachings, and was affected more than I knew by the language of the King James Version, which is the translation I still prefer. For most of my adult life I have been an urgently interested and frequently uneasy reader of the Bible, particularly of the Gospels. At the same time I have tried to be a worthy reader of Dante, Milton,

*Written originally as a speech for the first joint convocation of the Lexington Theological Seminary and the Baptist Seminary of Kentucky, Lexington, Kentucky, August 30, 2005.

Herbert, Blake, Eliot, and other poets of the Christian tradition. As a result of this reading and of my experience, I am by principle and often spontaneously, as if by nature, a man of faith. But my reading of the Gospels, comforting and clarifying and instructive as they frequently are, deeply moving or exhilarating as they frequently are, has caused me to understand them also as a burden, sometimes raising the hardest of personal questions, sometimes bewildering, sometimes contradictory, sometimes apparently outrageous in their demands. This is the confession of an unconfident reader.

I will begin by dealing with the embarrassing questions that the Gospels impose, I imagine, upon any serious reader. There are two of these, and the first is this: If you had been living in Jesus's time and had heard Him teaching, would you have been one of His followers? To be an honest taker of this test, I think you have to try to forget that you have read the Gospels and that Jesus has been a "big name" for two thousand years. You have to imagine instead that you are walking past the local courthouse and you come upon a crowd listening to a man named Joe Green or Green Joe, depending on judgments whispered among the listeners on the fringe. You too stop to listen, and you soon realize that Joe Green is saying something utterly scandalous, utterly unexpectable from the premises of modern society. He is saying: "Don't resist evil. If somebody slaps your right cheek, let him slap your left cheek too. Love your enemies. When people curse you, you must bless them. When people hate you, you must treat them kindly. When people mistrust you, you must pray for them. This is the way you must act if you want to be children of God." Well, you know how happily *that* would be received, not only in the White House and the Capitol, but among most of your neighbors. And then suppose this Joe Green looks at you over the heads of the crowd, calls you by name, and says, "I want to come to dinner at your house."

I suppose that you, like me, hope very much that you would say, "Come ahead." But I suppose also that you, like me, had better not be too sure. You will remember that in Jesus's lifetime even His most intimate friends could hardly be described as overconfident.

The second question is this—it comes right after the verse in which Jesus says, "If you love me, keep my commandments." Can you be sure that you would keep His commandments if it became excruciatingly painful to do so? And here I need to tell another story, this time one that actually happened.

In 1569, in Holland, a Mennonite named Dirk Willems, under threat of capital sentence as a heretic, was fleeing from arrest, pursued by a "thief catcher." As they ran across a frozen body of water, the thief-catcher broke through the ice. Without help, he would have drowned. What did Dirk Willems do then?

Was the thief-catcher an enemy merely to be hated, or was he a neighbor to be loved as one loves oneself? Was he an enemy whom one must love in order to be a child of God? Was he "one of the least of these my brethren"?

What Dirk Willems did was turn back, put out his hands to his pursuer, and save his life. The thief-catcher, who then of course wanted to let his rescuer go, was forced to arrest him. Dirk Willems was brought to trial, sentenced, and burned to death by a "lingering fire."

I, and I suppose you, would like to be a child of God even at the cost of so much pain. But would we, in similar circumstances, turn back to offer the charity of Christ to an enemy? Again, I don't think we ought to be too sure. We should remember that "Christian" generals and heads of state have routinely thanked God for the deaths of their enemies, and that the persecutors of 1569 undoubtedly thanked God for the capture and death of the "heretic" Dirk Willems.

Those are peculiar questions. I don't think we can escape them, if we are honest. And if we are honest, I don't think we can answer them. We humans, as we well know, have repeatedly been surprised by what we will or won't do under pressure. A person may come to be, as many have been, heroically faithful in great adversity, but as long as that person is alive we can only say that he or she did well but remains under the requirement to *do* well. As long as we are alive, there is always a next time, and so the questions remain. These are questions we must live with, regarding them as unanswerable and yet profoundly influential.

-------◆--------

The other burdening problems of the Gospels that I want to talk about are like those questions in that they are not solvable but can only be lived with as a sort of continuing education. These problems, however, are not so personal or dramatic but are merely issues of reading and making sense.

As a reader, I am unavoidably a writer. Many years of trying to write what I have perceived to be true have taught me that there are limits to what a human mind can know, and limits to what a human language can say. One may believe, as I do, in inspiration, but one must believe knowing that even the most inspired are limited in what they can tell of what they know. We humans write and read, teach and learn, at the inevitable cost of falling short. The language that reveals also obscures. And these qualifications that bear on any writing must bear of course on the Gospels.

I need to say also that, as a reader, I am first of all a literalist, as I think every reader should be. This does not mean that I don't appreciate Jesus's occasional irony or sarcasm ("They have their reward"), or that I am against interpretation, or that I don't believe in "higher levels of meaning." It certainly does not mean that I think every word of the Bible is equally true, or that "literalist" is a synonym for "fundamentalist." I mean simply that I expect any writing to make literal sense before making sense of any other kind. Interpretation should not contradict or otherwise violate the literal meaning. To read the Gospels as a literalist is, to me, the way to take them as seriously as possible.

But to take the Gospels seriously, to assume that they say what they mean and mean what they say, is the beginning of troubles. Those would-be literalists who yet argue that the Bible is unerring and unquestionable have not dealt with its contradictions, which of course it does contain, and the Gospels are not exempt. Some of Jesus's instructions are burdensome, not because they involve contradiction, but merely because they are so demanding. The proposition that love, forgiveness, and peaceableness are the only neighborly relationships that are acceptable to God is difficult for us weak and violent humans, but it is plain enough for any literalist. We must either accept it as an absolute or absolutely reject it. The same for the proposition that we are not permitted to choose our neighbors ahead of time or to limit neighborhood, as is plain from the parable of the Samaritan. The same for the requirement that we must be perfect, like God, which seems as outrageous as the Buddhist vow to "save all sentient beings," and perhaps is meant to measure and instruct us in the same way. It is, to say the least, unambiguous.

But what, for example, are we to make of Luke 14:26: "If any man come to me, and hate not his father, and mother, and wife, and children, and brethren, and sisters, yea, and his own life also, he cannot be my disciple." This contradicts not only the fifth commandment but Jesus's own instruction to "Love thy neighbor as thyself." It contradicts His obedience to his mother at the marriage in Cana of Galilee. It contradicts the concern He shows for the relatives of his friends and followers. But the word in the King James Version is "hate." If you go to the New English Bible or the New Revised Standard Version, looking for relief, the word still is "hate." This clearly is the sort of thing that leads to "biblical exegesis." My own temptation is to become a literary critic, wag my head learnedly, and say, "Well, this obviously is a bit of hyperbole—the sort of exaggeration a teacher would use to shock his students awake." Maybe so, but it is not obviously so, and it comes perilously close to "He didn't really mean it"—always a risky assumption when reading, and especially dangerous when reading the Gospels. Another possibility, and I think a better one, is to accept our failure to understand, not as a misstatement or a textual flaw or as a problem to be solved, but as a question to live with and a burden to be borne.

We may say with some reason that such apparent difficulties might be resolved if we knew more, a further difficulty being that we *don't* know more. The Gospels, like all other written works, impose on their readers the burden of their incompleteness. However partial we may be to the doctrine of the true account or "realism," we must concede at last that reality is inconceivably great and any representation of it necessarily incomplete.

St. John at the end of his Gospel, remembering perhaps the third verse of his first chapter, makes a charming acknowledgement of this necessary incompleteness: "And there are also many other things which Jesus did, the which, if they should be written every one, I suppose that even the world itself could not contain the books that should be written." Our darkness, then, is not going to be completely lighted. Our ignorance finally is irremediable. We humans are never going to know everything, even assuming we have the capacity, because for reasons of the most insistent practicality we can't be told everything. We need to remember here Jesus's repeated admonitions to his disciples: You don't know; you don't understand; you've got it wrong.

The Gospels, then, stand at the opening of a mystery in which our lives are deeply, dangerously, and inescapably involved. This is a mystery that the Gospels can only partially reveal, for it could be fully revealed only by more books than the world could contain. It is a mystery that we are condemned but also are highly privileged to live our way into, trusting properly that to our little knowledge greater knowledge may be revealed. It is this privilege that should make us wary of any attempt to reduce faith to a rigmarole of judgments and explanations, or to any sort of familiar talk about God. Reductive religion is just as objectionable as reductive science, and for the same reason: Reality is large, and our minds are small.

--------◆--------

And so the issue of reality—What is the *scope* of reality? What is real?—emerges as the crisis of this discussion. Right at the heart of the religious impulse there seems to be a certain solicitude for reality: the fear of foreclosing it or of reducing it to some merely human estimate. Many of us are still refusing to trust Caesar, in any of his modern incarnations, with the power to define reality. Many of us are still refusing to entrust that power to science. As inhabitants of the modern world, we are religious now perhaps to the extent of our desire to crack open the coffin of materialism, and to give to reality a larger, freer definition than is allowed by the militant materialists of the corporate economy and their political servants, or by the mechanical paradigm of reductive science. Or perhaps I can make most plain what I'm trying to get at if I say that many of us are still withholding credence, just as properly and for the same reasons, from any person or institution claiming to have the definitive word on the purposes and the mind of God.

It seems to me that all the religions I know anything about emerge from an instinct to push against any merely human constraints on reality. In the Bible such constraints are conventionally attributed to "the world" in the pejorative sense of that term, which we may define as the world of the creation *reduced* by any of the purposes of selfishness. The contrary purpose, the purpose of freedom, is stated by Jesus in the fourth Gospel: "I am come that they might have life, and that they might have it more abundantly."

This astonishing statement can be thought about and understood endlessly, for it is endlessly meaningful, but I don't think it calls for much in the way of interpretation. It does call for a very strict and careful reading of the word "life."

To talk about or to desire more abundance of anything has probably always been dangerous, but it seems particularly dangerous now. In an age of materialist science, economics, art, and politics, we ought not to be much shocked by the appearance of materialist religion. We know we don't have to look far to find people who equate more abundant life with a bigger car, a bigger house, a bigger bank account, and a bigger church. They are wrong, of course. If Jesus meant only that we should have more possessions or even more "life expectancy," then John 10:10 is no more remarkable than an advertisement for any commodity whatever. Abundance, in this verse, cannot refer to an abundance of material possessions, for life does not require a material abundance; it requires only a material sufficiency. That sufficiency granted, life itself, which is a membership in the living world, is already an abundance.

But even life in this generous sense of membership in creation does not protect us, as we know, from the dangers of avarice, of selfishness, of the wrong kind of abundance. Those dangers can be overcome only by the realization that in speaking of more abundant life, Jesus is not proposing to free *us* by making us richer; he is proposing to set *life* free from precisely that sort of error. He is talking about life, which is only incidentally our life, as a limitless reality.

---------◆---------

Now that I have come out against materialism, I fear that I will be expected to say something in favor of spirituality. But if I am going to go on in the direction of what Jesus meant by "life" and "more abundantly," then I have got to avoid that duality of matter and spirit at all costs.

As every reader knows, the Gospels are overwhelmingly concerned with the conduct of human life, of life in the human commonwealth. In the Sermon on the Mount and in other places Jesus is asking his followers to see that the way to more abundant life is the way of love. We are to love one another, and this love is to be more comprehensive than our love for family and friends and tribe and nation. We are to love our neighbors though they may be strangers to us. We are to love our enemies. And this is to be a practical love; it is to be practiced, here and now. Love evidently is not just a feeling but is indistinguishable from the willingness to help, to be useful to one another. The way of love is indistinguishable, moreover, from the way of freedom. We don't need much imagination to imagine that to be free of hatred, of enmity, of the endless and hopeless effort to oppose violence with violence, would be to have life more abundantly. To be free of indifference would be to have life more abundantly. To be free of the insane rationalizations for our desire to kill one another—that surely would be to have life more abundantly.

And where more than in the Gospels' teaching about love do we see that famously estranged pair, matter and spirit, melt and flow together? There was a Samaritan who came upon one of his enemies, a Jew, lying wounded beside the road. And the Samaritan had compassion on the Jew and bound up his wounds and took care of him. Was this help spiritual or material? Was the Samaritan's compassion earthly or heavenly? If those questions confuse us, that is only because we have for so long allowed ourselves to believe, as if to divide reality impartially between science and religion, that

material life and spiritual life, earthly life and heavenly life, are two different things.

To get unconfused, let us go to a further and even more interesting question about the parable of the Samaritan: Why? Why did the Samaritan
reach out in love to his enemy, a Jew, who happened also to be his neighbor? Why was the unbounding of this love so important to Jesus?

We might reasonably answer, remembering Genesis 1:27, that all
humans, friends and enemies alike, have the same dignity, deserve the
same respect, and are worthy of the same compassion because they are, all
alike, made in God's image. That is enough of a mystery, and it implies
enough obligation, to waylay us a while. It is certainly something we need
to bear anxiously in mind. But it is also too human-centered, too potentially egotistical, to leave alone.

I think Jesus recommended the Samaritan's loving-kindness, what certain older writers called "holy living," simply as a matter of propriety, for
the Samaritan was living in what Jesus understood to be a holy world. The
foreground of the Gospels is occupied by human beings and the issues of
their connection to one another and to God. But there is a background,
and the background more often than not is the world in the best sense of
the word, the world as made, approved, loved, sustained, and finally to be
redeemed by God. Much of the action and the talk of the Gospels takes
place outdoors: on mountainsides, lake shores, river banks, in fields and
pastures, places populated not only by humans but by animals and plants,
both domestic and wild. And these non-human creatures, sheep and lilies
and birds, are always represented as worthy of, or as flourishing within, the
love and the care of God.

To know what to make of this, we need to look back to the Old Testament, to Genesis, to the Psalms, to the preoccupation with the relation of
the Israelites to their land that runs through the whole lineage of the
prophets. Through all this, much is implied or taken for granted. In only
two places that I remember is the always implicit relation—the practical or
working relation—of God to the creation plainly stated. Psalm 104:30,
addressing God and speaking of the creatures, says, "Thou sendest forth

thy spirit, they are created . . ." And, as if in response, Elihu says to Job (34:14–15) that if God "gather unto himself his spirit and his breath; All flesh shall perish together . . ." I have cut Elihu's sentence a little short so as to leave the emphasis on the phrase "all flesh."

Those also are verses that don't require interpretation, but I want to stretch them out in paraphrase just to make as plain as possible my reason for quoting them. They are saying that not just humans but *all* creatures live by participating in the life of God, by partaking of His spirit and breathing His breath.* And so the Samaritan reaches out in love to help his enemy, breaking all the customary boundaries, because he has clearly seen in his enemy not only a neighbor, not only a fellow human or a fellow creature, but a fellow sharer in the life of God.

When Jesus speaks of having life more abundantly, this, I think, is the life He means: a life that is not reducible by division, category, or degree, but is one thing, heavenly and earthly, spiritual and material, divided only insofar as it is embodied in distinct creatures. He is talking about a finite world that is infinitely holy, a world of time that is filled with life that is eternal. His offer of more abundant life, then, is not an invitation to declare ourselves as certified "Christians," but rather to become conscious, consenting, and responsible participants in the one great life, a fulfillment hardly institutional at all.

To be convinced of the sanctity of the world, and to be mindful of a human vocation to responsible membership in such a world, must always have been a burden. But it is a burden that falls with greatest weight on us humans of the industrial age who have been and are, by any measure, the humans most guilty of desecrating the world and of destroying creation. And we ought to be a little terrified to realize that, for the most part and at least for the time being, we are helplessly guilty. It seems as though industrial humanity has brought about phase two of original sin. We all are now

---

*We now know that this relationship is even more complex, more utterly inclusive and whole, than the biblical writers suspected. Some scientists would insist that the conventional priority given to living creatures over the nonliving is misleading. Try, for example, to separate life from the lifeless minerals on which it depends.

complicit in the murder of creation. We certainly do know how to apply better measures to our conduct and our work. We know how to do far better than we are doing. But we don't know how to extricate ourselves from our complicity very surely or very soon. How could we live without degrading our soils, slaughtering our forests, polluting our streams, poisoning the air and the rain? How could we live without the ozone hole and the hypoxic zones? How could we live without endangering species, including our own? How could we live without the war economy and the holocaust of the fossil fuels? To the offer of more abundant life, we have chosen to respond with the economics of extinction.

If we take the Gospels seriously, we are left, in our dire predicament, facing an utterly humbling question: How must we live and work so as not to be estranged from God's presence in His work and in all His creatures? The answer, we may say, is given in Jesus's teaching about love. But that answer raises another question that plunges us into the abyss of our ignorance, which is both human and peculiarly modern: How are we to make of that love an economic practice?

That question calls for many answers, and we don't know most of them. It is a question that those humans who want to answer will be living and working with for a long time—if they are allowed a long time. Meanwhile, may Heaven guard us from those who think they already have the answers.

(2005)

Part III

Letter to Daniel Kemmis

Dear Daniel,

You have written to me out of your concern for the future of the Democratic Party. Because I respect you, and because I hang onto my hope that a principled and serious politics is still possible in these United States, I want to risk a reply. For what it may be worth, I will tell you my thoughts about the failure of the Party, and about the issues I think are involved. Why not just give up on the Democratic Party? Well, because of its name.

The first problem, I think, is the priority the Democrats have given to winning. This is understandable, humanly speaking, but politically it is the main reason our public dialogue has now been reduced to "spin"—a compound of clichés and falsehoods. We are all for freedom and against tyranny—but such declarations fall far short of our need to speak and act with intelligence. "Me too" is not an adequate response to economic globalization, the war in Iraq, "toughness," etc. The first responsibility of a candidate is not to win an election but to respond intelligently to the issues, even at the cost of losing.

For example, the failure or refusal of the Democrats to speak intelligently in public has permitted the Bush Republicans to capture the flags of religion and morality—and to do so on terms utterly bogus and by appealing to the low instincts of self-righteousness, pride, and anger. And so I will deal with the issues of religion and morality first.

The religion most in question, because most useful in hostage to politics, is Christianity. And this leads us straight into the red–blue division, which I

DANIEL KEMMIS is a former Minority Leader and Speaker of the Montana House of Representatives, and a former mayor of Missoula. He is the author of *This Sovereign Land: A New Vision for Governing the West.*

think the media have exaggerated but which nevertheless exists and is significant. It is a fact that a lot of liberal intellectuals think there is a necessary conflict between science and religion, that religious faith has been defeated or disproved by science, and that therefore one cannot be intelligently religious or an intelligent Christian. This starts "high up" in the universities and the liberal journals, but it trickles down, along with the inclination to gloat over the supposed victory and condescend to the supposedly defeated.

The stereotypical "liberal" view of the religious people of the "red states" is that they are provincial and stupid. This overlooks the possibility that there is such a thing as an intelligent Christian, and such a thing even as an intelligent fundamentalist Christian—intelligent enough at least to recognize "liberal" condescension or contempt and to resent it.

Behind that error is another, perhaps more important, and that is the assumption that modern science is somehow contrary to Genesis and disproves it. The quarrel between evolution and creationism seems to be taking place in a world utterly devoid of imagination, in which supposedly learned intellectuals and the most fundamental fundamentalists read Genesis with equal literalness and simplicity of mind.

Genesis, of course, cannot be disproved by modern science, any more than modern science can be disproved by Genesis. The biblical story of creation and the science of evolution come from two radically different kinds of thought—or two different kinds, even, of consciousness. The early chapters of Genesis welled up out of the deepest reaches of human imagination and inspiration. They tell a story of great sanctity and beauty that has resonated through our culture for thousands of years. As a not overly qualified supposer, I suppose that all of us ought to know this story and heed its warnings. Evolutionary science, on the contrary, is rational and empirical, excluding by principle the sort of genius that gave us the Genesis story. Like all science, it is an attempt to deal with evidence that is available, and to limit itself to that evidence. I suppose also that we need to know about this science, which, like Genesis, has important things to tell us about our relation to this world—and which, intelligent as we may be, we have not much applied to our way of living in this world. We don't, by policy, apply the evolutionary requirement of local adaptation to any economic activity that I know of.

I venture to say that no young mind is going to be seriously warped by exposure either to Genesis or to the theory of evolution. If I had children in school, I would prefer that they should be taught both. But I would prefer that they should be taught intelligently about Genesis rather than unintelligently about evolution—and vice versa. I would say moreover that a governmental requirement to teach *only* one or the other is not consistent either with freedom or with the dignity of teaching.

--------◆--------

If I am right in assuming that it is possible to be an intelligent Christian, then the Democrats' failure to appeal to intelligent Christians is a serious mistake. I don't mean at all to say that religious faith should be made a political issue. We have been well advised, and by some Christians, that religion should not be put at the disposal of politics; God should not be enlisted to campaign for Caesar. And it seems extremely doubtful that, under present circumstances, there can be such a thing as a Christian government. Nevertheless, the political virtues of honesty, charity, good stewardship, forgiveness of enemies, peaceableness, temperance, justice, and mercy all have very firm support in the Gospels. It was therefore foolish for Democrats to stand dumbfounded while the Bush Republicans campaigned as God's own party.

One problem with making religion the servant of politics, obviously, is that it oversimplifies religion. Another problem is that it oversimplifies politics. It is surely because of the moral timidity or incompetence of the Democrats that the Republicans have been able to reduce the issues of "values" to a mere three: evolution, abortion, and homosexuality. I have spoken of evolution. Now I will speak of the other two.

I must admit that I am opposed to abortion except as a last resort to save a pregnant woman's life. The crucial question raised by this practice is: What is killed? The answer can only be: A human being. If you have trouble believing that the situation is at all changed by calling this being an embryo or a fetus, then you can see why a lot of people find the practice repugnant, and *not* because they are backward, ignorant, malevolent, or stupid. That a lot of people find it repugnant, and therefore cannot defend or excuse it as a "right," is a political fact that the Democrats are going to have to come to terms with, even though this seems to be an issue that cannot be much moved one way or another by argument. The division appears simply to be between people who are not much troubled by the killing of a fetus and people who are very much troubled by the killing of an unborn baby. I can allow that some people may be able to support abortion "in conscience," but that does not excuse them from acknowledging its violence, its moral difficulty, and its emotional hardship for the women (and perhaps the men too) who are involved. An abortion is not simply a "medical procedure." If it is a "right," it certainly is far more complicated and burdened than, say, the right to speak freely or assemble peaceably. If they can do nothing else, these opponents need to understand one another. It is not overly difficult to imagine either the repugnance with which some regard the killing, or circumstances in which abortion might seem the best of two bad choices.

If abortion is not a right but a wrong, then it is wrong because it violates the "right to life" as set forth in the Declaration of Independence, and because it violates that "reverence for life" to which we are called by much instruction. If that right and that reverence apply to abortion, then they apply as well to capital punishment and to war, especially to the killing of innocent women, children, and old people in war. There is no consistency between "compassion" for the unborn and "toughness" toward the deliberate killing of the born, just as there is no consistency between opposition to the callous use of lethal violence against the born and a "liberal" indifference to the rights of the unborn.

--------·--------

The Democratic Party has been further weakened by mishandling the issue of homosexuality. It seems to be a sort of folklore of liberalism that any group that has suffered from a categorical disapproval should be compensated by a categorical approval. But this is nonsense. The reason that one can't reasonably approve of racial minorities or homosexuals is that one can't reasonably approve of racial majorities or heterosexuals. Or one had better not, considering that all categories of people include people who are not by any respectable standard approvable. Some homosexuals are good people; some are not. I suppose we should approve of the good ones and disapprove of the bad ones. Beyond that, I think we have to say that homosexuals should not be denied any human right on the basis of their category.

By raising the issue of homosexual marriage, by making it a *political* issue, I think homosexuals have done themselves and the rest of us a disservice: That is, they have invited the government to make a public judgment of people's private sexual behavior, which ought to be none of the government's business, so long as the behavior is not abusive of other people. Governmental approval of anybody's sexual behavior is as inappropriate and as offensive to freedom as governmental disapproval. The government's interest in people's living arrangements should go no further than "domestic partnerships," which ought to give the same legal protections and rights to widowed sisters or bachelor brothers or friends or "partners" living together as to married couples. Justice and (with luck) mercy should be the government's business. Let sacraments such as marriage be the business of religions and communities.

Until lately, anyhow, marriage was not thought to be a right. It was a requirement, a part of the communal means, often misled or ignored, of sexual responsibility.

But it ought to be obvious to every sane person in both parties, in both the blue states and the red ones, that opposition to evolution, abortion, and homosexual marriage does not constitute an adequate religion. It does not constitute even an adequate set of "values."

The great moral issue of our time, too much ignored by both sides of our present political division, is violence. From the colonialism that began with long-distance navigation to the present stage of industrialism, we of the so-called West have lived and gathered wealth increasingly by violence. This has been increasingly an age of fire. We now travel and transport our goods by means of controlled explosions in the engines of our vehicles. We run our factories, businesses, and households by means of fires or controlled explosions in furnaces and power plants. We fight our wars by controlled, and sometimes uncontrolled, explosions. Violence, in short, is the norm of our economic life and our national security. The line that connects the bombing of a civilian population to the mountain "removed" by strip mining to the gullied and poisoned field to the clear-cut watershed to the tortured prisoner seems to run pretty straight.

We are living, it seems, into the culmination of a long warfare—at first merely commercial and then industrial, always unabashedly violent—against human beings and other creatures, and of course against the earth itself. The purpose of this warfare has been to render the real goods of the world into various forms of abstract wealth: money, gold, shares, etc. Just as technological power has increasingly served this purpose, so increasingly has political power.

The trouble with this is that it is bound to reduce the supply of real goods, the goods that sustain life: fertile soils, breathable air, drinkable water, food, and other essential materials that can come only from the native fertility of the living world. We are now, measurably, reducing the availability of these life-supporting goods that we can think of (though only on the conditions of good health and good care) as self-renewing or "sustainable." We are also destroying rapidly the supplies of the fossil fuels, which are limited and not renewable, and on which we have become totally dependent.

And so we may conclude that up to a point, and by a very low practical standard, violence "works." That is, it enables a person or a corporation or a nation to take whatever is valuable or desirable by the most direct means, however great the unaccounted costs. But eventually the violence that once gave us so readily, directly, and "cheaply" what we wanted begins to put the desirable things at an increasing distance from us, so that to get them requires always a longer reach and greater expense. At that point in its history, an extractive society begins to realize that, contrary to its old logic and expectations, it has in fact been weakened by its power and impoverished by its wealth. We are now at that point in the United States. Having burned petroleum more and more extravagantly for half a century, we are now finding the supply more distant, more limited, and consequently more costly. And having thoughtlessly polluted our streams and rivers, we have seen in recent years a rapidly growing market for bottled drinking water. I am sure that some will say that a rapidly growing market for water is "good for the economy," and most of us are still affluent enough to pay the cost. Nevertheless, it is a considerable cost that we are now paying for drinkable water, which we once had in plentiful supply at little cost or none at all. And the increasing of the cost suggests that the time may come when the cost will be unaffordable.

Meanwhile, our attempt to maintain a "growth economy" in a measurably diminishing world is playing the devil with our traditional (and admirable) moral code, which our most prominent politicians now put to public use mainly to paint over our immoral behavior. We make war, we are told, for the love of peace. We subvert our Bill of Rights and impose our will abroad for the sake of freedom and the rule of law. We honor greed and waste with the name of economy. We allow ever greater wealth and power to accumulate in the hands of a privileged few only to provide jobs for working people and charity to the poor. And we sanctify all this as Christian, though the Gospels support none of it by so much as a line or a word.

The violence underlying this hypocrisy is great, and so are the costs. The costs are economic, ecological, and political. Sooner or later, the increase of costs and better accounting are going to show that the costs are not affordable. Society's leaders and would-be leaders will have to learn and teach that violent solutions never pay their way, but invariably produce a net loss to the world, to humankind, and to freedom and the rule of law.

The economic costs of war, to use the most extreme example, are always paid at the sacrifice of real prosperity. The ecological costs of war are not even calculated; both sides readily sacrifice the health of nature to their emergencies. As for the political costs, we know that war depresses public dialogue and debate, enlarges executive power, diminishes citizens' rights, encourages governmental secrecy and deception, and deforms the outlines of human decency. Thus a government making war for the sake of peace, freedom, and human dignity—as it will never cease to declare—will curtail the rights of prisoners, resort to torture, deny its errors, exaggerate its virtues, demonize the enemy, and (as is inevitable in modern war) kill many innocent people, including, of course, many children. And we should never forget that it is easy for older people "doing their solemn duty" in the dignity and comfort of high office to send young soldiers into combat. Nor should we forget that the war industries never offer, and are never asked, to sacrifice any fraction of their profits to further a cause for which others are expected to sacrifice their lives.

(In a time when it is the fashion to propose amendments to the Constitution, I would like to propose an amendment requiring (1) that when war breaks out the president and all consenting members of his administration as well as all consenting legislators, whatever their ages, should immediately be enrolled as privates in combat units; and (2) that for the duration of any war all executives and shareholders of corporations contributing to the war effort should be restricted to the same annual income as the workers in their factories—no sacrifice being too great in a time of national peril.)

The effects of a violent economy are the same as the effects of war: the degradation of nature, the misuse of government, and, ultimately and inevitably, a net economic loss. As we now have it, the industrial economy operates as if, like an army in battle, it is in a perpetual state of emergency, requiring violence as the first resort and the sacrifice of precious and irreplaceable things. We can see too that at times war and the economy are exactly the same. Both are entirely directed to short-term gains regardless of the long-term costs. But let us dare to ask some long-term questions:

How long by a mere economic reckoning can we and our world afford the extravagance of industrial war? Is there actually some economic good in making and using massively destructive weapons and then building back again all the necessary things that they have destroyed? If deadly violence can in fact stop deadly violence, then why has deadly violence not stopped? Does such violence have some logic inherent in it that can stop it before everything is destroyed, or can it be stopped only by a logic that is external to it, a logic of peace? Since somebody has to stop it, if it is ever to be stopped, why don't we, the world's mightiest nation, stop it? Why don't we at least give some public attention and support to those means by which some potentially deadly conflicts have been solved without violence?

------◆------

The present economy, by means of its purchases of governmental power, weighs invariably against the natural world; against working people, small farmers, and locally-owned small businesses; and against the life, integrity, beauty, and dignity of communities, both rural and urban. It is destroying our country. And this has come to be very much a two-party economy. Its opponents are to be found, not in the offices of government, state or national, but in organizations of mere citizens, scattered and often at odds, often local and small, who are trying to remove the threat from something good.

These, I think, are the people a political party worthy of our respect and our votes will have to speak for. It will have to defend the health of ecosystems and watersheds. It will have to advocate the development of local economies: the interdependence of cities and towns with their adjoining landscapes of farms or ranches, gardens, forests, lakes and streams; the cooperation of farmers, ranchers, gardeners, foresters, fishermen, and other users of the land and water with homegrown, locally-owned, appropriately-scaled businesses that will process and distribute the local products. It will know and say that such economies, providing a significant measure of local self-sufficiency, are indispensable to the security of the nation. It will insist that the working people are not readily transportable or dispensable "resources" for industry, but instead are honored and necessary members of their communities, entitled to just wages, decent working conditions, and pleasant places to live. It will honor the idea of vocation: that young people should find the work to which they are called or are naturally suited, and, having found it, should be able to devote their lives to it. It will, in short, tell the truth about the human economy: Competitiveness, covetousness, ruthlessness, and greed are not economic virtues; the economic virtues are neighborliness, generosity, trust, good workmanship, thrift, and care. It will tell the truth also about war: We can no longer afford it, or bear it; we will have to think of better ways—good economic practice, honest talk, peaceable resistance—to protect the things needing to be protected. It will repudiate all narrow and special definitions of conservation, but will use the term in the broadest sense to mean giving care to everything needing care: wilderness, all bodies of water, the air, farms and working forests, all the creatures (living and not-living), neighbors, families and communities, languages, cultures, minds, souls, freedom, democracy, the Constitution.

This is one way of describing a party worth working and voting for, worth even being defeated for. What I have written is dismissible, I know, as "idealistic" or even as "a dream." But I believe it is practical, and demonstrably so, at every point.

Your Friend,
Wendell

Daniel Kemmis Replies

Dear Wendell,

Thanks for your letter on the fate and future of the Democratic Party. I will respond with a perspective from the western "red states." As a lifelong Democrat, concerned about the decline the Party had suffered throughout the interior West in the 1980s and 1990s, I have been working with a group called Democrats for the West to build sustainable Democratic majorities throughout the Rockies. I'm convinced that the West can and should be Democratic country. But how can that happen?

The good news is that it is happening already. It's true that at the presidential level, this region actually slipped further into the "red" column in 2004. New Mexico had voted for Al Gore in 2000, but in 2004, all eight states in the region—Arizona, New Mexico, Nevada, Utah, Colorado, Wyoming, Montana, and Idaho, voted for President Bush. But a quick look beneath that presidential veneer reveals a very different picture beginning to emerge in the region. In 2002, for example, there were no Democratic governors in the eight-state region; now half the governors are Democrats. We picked up a U.S. Senate seat and a congressional seat in Colorado in 2004, and Democrats gained control of both legislative houses in Montana and Colorado. So, there is change afoot in the Rockies, and it is change in a Democratic direction.

Still, to maintain that momentum, we have not only to be grasping temporary opportunities or leveraging Republican failures; we have to be presenting effective governing platforms that speak persuasively to solid majorities of our western neighbors. You ask, "Why not just give up on the

Democratic Party?" For years, that's exactly what too many westerners have been doing. To reverse that trend in a sustainable way, we need a clear, principled, cogent (and in our case western) answer to your question. And your starting point is exactly the same as mine: We can't give up on the Democratic Party "because of its name."

Most Democratic tacticians want to start somewhere else—somewhere that the polls or the focus groups or the spin-masters have pointed them. But your instinct for the importance of words leads you to the core of the matter. If the Democratic Party isn't fundamentally about democracy, then it has in fact lost its bearings.

For decades after Jefferson founded the party, it was known by friend and foe alike simply as "The Democracy"—a tribute to its stubborn insistence that the people had to be trusted with the task of governing themselves. I want to come back to that matter of trust because I think it's crucial to the fate of the Party still today, but first I want to drill a little deeper into the vein you have opened by invoking the Party's name.

The more there is at stake, the more sense it makes to go back to the beginning of things. That, I take it, is some part of your point in reminding us that Genesis is still, in some inexhaustible way, true. So are all the creation stories that survive the test of time, never losing their capacity to help us understand the often baffling and always challenging world we find ourselves inhabiting "east of Eden." It's in this same spirit that I think it is worthwhile, one more time, to go back to the beginning of the country's oldest surviving political party, to see what its genesis can still teach us—and especially what it can teach us about re-enlivening "The Democracy" out here in the "red states."

I first encountered your work early in my political career, when I was on my way to becoming the Democratic floor leader of the Montana House of Representatives. I was trying to understand what there was in my experience of growing up on a small dryland farm in eastern Montana that could help broaden the message of Montana Democrats at least enough to give us a majority in the Legislature. We did win that majority, enabling me to move from the Minority Leader's to the Speaker's office, and we did it in part by winning back some seats in the rural part of the state where my great-grandparents had homesteaded in the 1880s.

When I first read *The Unsettling of America*, I found a clarifying retelling of my family's story, and (between the lines) a retelling of the Democratic Party's story. Your book was not in any sense a partisan work, but it was a deeply Jeffersonian one, and it helped me understand how fundamentally Jeffersonian had been the formative experiences of my childhood on the farm. Recalling how we and our neighbors depended on one another, how we built our barns, branded our calves, and put up our silage together, I understood, with your help, why Jefferson was so insistent on the link between democracy and small family farms.

The uncomplicated straightforwardness, the honesty, the reliability, the trust and the trustworthiness that bound us to our neighbors and that literally enabled us to survive on that forbidding landscape had, to my childish perception, simply been how things were. But your book, alongside Robert Bellah's *Habits of the Heart*, helped me understand that these life ways, growing naturally out of the struggle with hard country, were the same "civic virtues" that Jefferson had thought were indispensable to the enterprise of democracy.

So now, as The Democracy seeks once again to build strength in the rural reaches of the country, and as it struggles with how to speak "values language," my instincts are to return to the source and ask once again what living lessons we can draw from the Party's own genesis.

The Democratic Party was born out of a firm conviction that democracy depends on old-fashioned virtues and values, and that people making their living off the land were the ones most likely to have incorporated those virtues and values into their lives. But can these origins still possibly have any relevance at a time when only a tiny and still shrinking fraction of Americans make their living directly off the earth? Don't we now need to look for some entirely different grounding for The Democracy?

We certainly have to be adaptive to changing times, and nowhere is that more true than here in the West, which is in many ways the most rapidly changing region in the country.

We're seeing, for example, the emergence of a whole new western economy, where ecological integrity and community livability are rapidly replacing extractive activities as the region's prime economic assets. No region of the country is learning more quickly or more painfully what you mean when you describe how "an extractive society begins to realize that, contrary to its old logic and expectations, it has in fact been weakened by its power and impoverished by its wealth." Coming to terms with these changes is hard and vexing work. It has reminded me more than once of a line from one of your poems to the effect that in the kind of country both you and I inhabit, "Its hardship is its possibility."

The arid, interior West has always been hard country, but its very ruggedness has selected and shaped a people that Jefferson would have recognized as the ideal raw material for democracy. Wallace Stegner put it in genuinely western language in his often quoted lines about this region:

> Angry as one may be at what heedless men have done and still do to a noble habitat, one cannot be pessimistic about the West. This is the native home of hope. When it fully learns that cooperation, not rugged individualism, is the quality that most characterizes and preserves it, then it will have achieved itself and outlived its origins. Then it has a chance to create a society to match its scenery.

The West is now busy "outliving its origins" and "achieving itself" in a number of ways. I've already mentioned the emergence of the new western economy, where ecological integrity and community livability have become the prime economic assets. But if westerners are outgrowing an era of ecological heedlessness, we're also beginning to outlive some of the human heedlessness, all too present in certain strains of the environmental movement.

As a westerner, I found myself agreeing strongly with your warning that Democrats too often appear to be condescending toward religious people of the red states. I'd only observe that it's not only on religious issues that Democrats have fallen into this trap. Here in the interior West, where public land and natural resource issues are paramount, the Democratic Party has been effectively tied in public perception with the "zero cut" and "cattle free" strand of environmentalism. This has made all too many farmers, ranchers, and loggers conclude that we as a party neither trust them with any stewardship responsibilities for their home landscapes, nor do we value the ways of life and communities they have built within those landscapes.

I actually know very few western Democrats who share in that condescension, but any western Democratic candidate must constantly battle that nationally-generated perception of what the "D" after our name implies. As western Democrats, we need the national party to give us room to articulate a genuinely western, genuinely democratic approach to the challenges and opportunities of this region. I'm encouraged by the conviction that our new national chairman, Howard Dean, understands this.

As a Democrat, I am vastly encouraged by the fact that westerners are starting to learn that it's possible to avoid the old excesses of clear-cutting and overgrazing, while still allowing rural communities to prosper through genuinely sustainable logging and ranching practices. And we're learning it just as Stegner said we would: by grasping that cooperation is an indispensable way of doing business if we hope to prosper in this hard country. That slow, incremental learning is revitalizing across the West those civic virtues that Jefferson saw as the core of The Democracy.

All across the West, especially on public land and natural resource issues, old enemies are learning new skills of solving together the problems of living in hard country. That kind of cooperation requires people to think harder, better, more creatively, to reach beyond themselves, to transcend what they already know and comfortably believe. It requires people to ask honest, open questions, and to come up with lasting solutions. It requires them to listen closely and actively to people they have never liked or trusted, to find a mutually beneficial solution. And the amazing thing is that it works. There are failures, of course, but people are finding that very often they can create something effective and lasting, not only on the ground but within and among themselves. Solving tough problems together forces people to reach beyond their narrow selves and enables them to discover together a wisdom they do not have as individuals. That, it seems to me, is the absolute essence of being a democratic people.

If there are key ingredients that make this kind of face-to-face democracy work, then two of them are honesty and trust. And if The Democracy is to send deep roots into these western landscapes, it will have to do it by speaking honestly and by building trust.

As Democrats scramble to find some newly effective way to address values, morals, and religion, there is a real danger that cleverness will outpace honesty. There are probably many clever ways to "frame the values discussion," but in the long run, the only strategy that can work is to speak the simple truth, as well as we may be able to discern it.

Jefferson's vision of democracy rested implicitly on the cultivation of old-fashioned values and virtues. In Jefferson's view of the world, those values and virtues came almost literally up out of the ground. When we examine them, we find that they consistently correspond closely with the core teachings of the great religious traditions—and especially with those of our Judaeo-Christian heritage. Perhaps it is no accident that so many of our religious teachings have the very earth of their origins clinging to them—whether it is the soil of Cain's garden, or that of the land of milk and honey, or the Christian faith that is so very like the planting and sprouting of seeds as to be all but indistinguishable from it. The teachings that stick through the generations and still sustain our faith seem so often to be the ones that remind us of our own struggles with hard but life-giving, faith-sustaining places.

In 1972, the people of Montana adopted a new state constitution. When it came time to write its preamble, there was at first an assumption that we should stick with the old preamble, which in turn had been patterned on the preamble to the U.S. Constitution. But then the framers thought about who Montanans had become after generations of building communities and raising families on these beloved, demanding landscapes. So they began their preamble with these words: "We the people of Montana, grateful to God for the quiet beauty of our state, the grandeur of its mountains, the vastness of its rolling plains...." We were, in other words, a grateful people, a hopeful people, a people ready to take on the task of governing ourselves. It isn't easy. It won't ever be easy. But its hardship is its possibility.

My childhood experience of close cooperation with our rural neighbors taught me that, when it came to dealing with the challenges of hard country, listening was as important as talking. I learned that democracy is not arrogant. It is humble. It respects the other—seriously, deeply, and dangerously—because the other if listened to genuinely might just turn out to be right. This I take to be your meaning when you say that on the religious issues that so deeply divide us, "If they can do nothing else, these opponents need to understand one another."

I have no illusions about how deep-seated and toxic our religious differences can be. Nor do I believe that we are likely to put them all behind us. But I do believe that we will begin to move off dead-center on an issue like abortion when people on both sides of the issue begin to do what westerners are now doing with increasing frequency on ecological issues. Just as people have found that they can reduce ecological damage while preserving valued ways of life, so I believe we will begin to see people of good will on both sides of the abortion debate fashioning ways of working together openly, non-coercively and nonviolently, to reduce steadily and significantly the number of unwanted pregnancies and the number of abortions. That is a goal a self-confident, empowered citizenry can achieve.

My experience as mayor of Missoula, Montana, left me convinced that today's West is practically bursting at the seams with creative, constructive, can-do democratic energy. Collaborative efforts are yielding great results. All across the West, people are working with one another to make their communities more livable, more attractive, more prosperous. They work together on trail systems, streamside restoration projects, performing arts centers, music festivals, land trusts, farmers' markets, skateboard parks, health clinics for the uninsured, downtown revitalization, and on and on and on.

Yet the Democratic Party has become so accustomed to thinking solely in terms of its standard constituency politics that this amazing democratic bonanza almost never shows up on the Party's radar screen.

A little remembering of the Party's proud history could help us overcome that myopia. The Democratic Party achieved its identity and its governing legitimacy by vigorously and stubbornly espousing the capacity of ordinary people to tackle together the problems they face. Jefferson was acutely aware that the enterprise of democracy—of people collectively governing their lives and shaping their world—was both a risky and a satisfying undertaking. If there is a key to the long life of the Democratic Party, it may lie in the fact that the democratic shaping of a world is such an invigorating and ennobling enterprise. People become fuller, more creative, and more dignified when they assume responsibility for governing themselves.

That's where my democratic faith continues to be rooted. I believe that, in the long run, good people learn to transcend their differences, not by out-arguing each other, but by realizing together the possibilities of hard country. That's where real, lasting, uniting values come from. I think that's why Thomas Jefferson was so convinced that people making their living off the earth were the backbone of The Democracy. They should be again.

Faithfully yours,
Daniel Kemmis

The Working Wilderness:
A Call for a Land Health Movement

BY COURTNEY WHITE

I have asked Courtney White to lend his essay, "The Working Wilderness," to this collection for three reasons:

First, I think it is a good essay.

Second, it tells of a serious and continuing effort on the part of some ranchers and conservationists to develop local knowledge sufficient to support a locally adapted land economy. This is an effort that is needed simply because it is necessary. If humans don't learn to adapt their land economies to the nature of their places, that will be a disaster, first for their places and then for the humans.

Third, it is an essay about cooperation between people and nature, between people and their places, and between ranchers and conservationists. This, again, is necessary. The only possible result of the human effort to "conquer" nature and one another is human defeat. The longstanding conflict between ranchers and conservationists is not only hopeless and ruinous for both; it is, as Daniel Kemmis points out, outmoded: "Cooperation is an indispensable way of doing business if we hope to prosper in this hard country."

Courtney and I know, of course, that some people are going to disagree with his thoughts, as some will disagree with mine. As essayists, we know that the purpose of an essay is not to deliver the final word. An essay's purpose is merely to take part in a conversation. So let the disagreements come. Long live the conversation! —W.B.

COURTNEY WHITE is cofounder and executive director of The Quivira Coalition, a nonprofit organization dedicated to building bridges between ranchers, environmentalists, public land managers, scientists, and others. He and his family live in Santa Fe, New Mexico.

--------◆--------

"The only progress that counts is that on the actual landscape
*of the back forty." —*ALDO LEOPOLD

DURING A CONSERVATION TOUR of the well-managed U Bar Ranch near
Silver City, New Mexico, I was asked to say a few words about a map given
to me recently by a friend.

We were taking a break in the shade of a large piñion tree, and I rose a
bit reluctantly (the day being hot and the shade being deep) to explain that
the map was commissioned by an alliance of ranchers concerned about the
creep of urban sprawl into the 500,000-acre Altar Valley, located south of
Tucson, Arizona. The map was important, I told them, for what it measured: indicators of rangeland health.

Drawn up in multiple colors, the map expressed the intersection of three
variables: soil stability, biotic integrity, and hydrological function—soil,
grass, and water, in other words. The map displayed three conditions for
each variable: "Stable," "At Risk," and "Unstable." A color represented a
particular intersection. For example, deep red designated an unstable, or
unhealthy, condition for soil, grass (vegetation), and water, while deep
green represented stable for all three. Other colors represented conditions
between these extremes.

In the middle of the map was a privately owned ranch called the Palo
Alto, I told them. Visiting it recently, I was shocked by its condition. It had
been overgrazed by cattle to the point of being nearly totally "cowburnt,"
to use author Ed Abbey's famous phrase. As one might expect, the color of
the Palo Alto on the map was blood red and there was plenty of it.

I paused briefly—now came the controversial part. This big splotch of
deep red continued well below the southern boundary of the Palo Alto, I
said. However, this was not a ranch. This was the Buenos Aires National
Wildlife Refuge, a large chunk of protected land that had been cattle-free
for nearly sixteen years....

That was as far as I got. Taking offense at the suggestion that the refuge might be ecologically unfit, a combative young environmentalist from Tucson cut me off. She knew the refuge, she explained, having worked hard to help "heal" it from decades of abuse by cows.

I countered by explaining that the map did not blame anyone for current conditions; nor did it offer opinions on any particular remedy. All it did was ask a simple question: Is the land functioning properly at the fundamental level of soil, grass, and water? For a portion of the Buenos Aires National Wildlife Refuge the answer was "no." For portions of the adjacent privately owned ranches, which were deep green on the map, the answer was "yes."

Why was that a problem?

I knew why. I had strayed too closely to a core belief of my fellow conservationists—that "protected" areas, such as national parks, wilderness areas, and wildlife refuges, must always rate, by definition, as being in better ecological condition than adjacent "working" landscapes.

Yet the Altar Valley map challenged this paradigm at a fundamental level, and when the tour commenced again, on a ranch that would undoubtedly encompass more deep greens than deep reds on a similar map, I saw in the reaction of the young activist a need to rethink the conservation movement in the American West.

From the ground up.

KNOWLEDGE

My conviction received a boost a few weeks later while sitting around a campfire after a tour of the CS Ranch. I was thinking about ethics. I believed at the time, as many conservationists still do, that the chore of ending overgrazing by cattle in the West was a matter of getting ranchers to adopt an ecological ethic along the lines suggested by Aldo Leopold in his famous "Land Ethic" essay, where he argued that humans had a moral obligation to be good stewards of nature.

The question, it seemed to me, was how to accomplish this lofty goal.

I decided to ask Julia Davis-Stafford, our host, for advice. Years ago, Julia and her sister, Kim, talked their family into switching to progressive ranch management on the magnificent 100,000-acre CS, located in northeastern New Mexico. It was a decision that over time caused the ranch to flourish economically and ecologically. In fact, the idea for my query came earlier in the day when I couldn't decide which was more impressive: the sight of a new beaver dam on the ranch or Julia's strong support for its presence.

The Davis family, it seemed to me, had embraced Leopold's land ethic big time. So, over the crackle of the campfire, I asked Julia, "How do we get other ranchers to change their ethics, too?"

Her answer altered everything I had been thinking up until that moment.

"We didn't change our ethics," she replied. "We're the same people we were fifteen years ago. What changed was our knowledge. We went back to school, in a sense, and we came back to the ranch with new ideas."

Knowledge, I suddenly realized, more than ethics, is the key to good land stewardship. Her point confirmed what I had observed during many visits to livestock operations across the region: Ranchers *do* have an environmental ethic, as they have claimed for so long. Often their ethic is a powerful one. What many lack, however, is new knowledge.

The same thing is true of many conservationists. In the years since I became an activist, starting as a Sierra Club volunteer and later co-founding a nonprofit organization dedicated to bridge-building between ranchers, environmentalists, and others, I came to the conclusion that it had obviously been a long time since any of us was in school. This is a problem because land management knowledge, like any knowledge, does not sit still for very long.

If conservationists could go back to school, as the Davis family did, what would we learn? Aldo Leopold had an idea: the fundamental principle of land health, which he described as "the capacity of the land for self-renewal." He also described conservation as "our effort to understand and preserve this capacity."

By studying the elements of land health, conservationists could learn that grazing is a natural process. The consumption of grass by ungulates has been going on in North America for at least sixty-six million years—

not by cattle, of course, but because they are domesticated animals they can be managed in a way that mimics the behavior of bison, recreating a relationship between grass and grazer that can be ecologically sustainable.

We could also learn that many landscapes need periodic pulses of energy, in the form of natural disturbance, to keep things vibrant. Many conservationists know that "cool" fires are a beneficial form of disturbance in ecosystems because they reduce tree density, burn up old grass, and aid nutrient cycling in the soil. But many of us don't know that small flood events can be a positive agent of change too, as can drought, wind storms, and even insect infestation. And nearly all of us fail (or refuse) to understand that animal impact caused by grazers, including cattle, can be a natural form of disturbance as well.

We could further learn, as the Davis family did, that the key to proper "disturbance" with cattle is to control the timing, intensity, and frequency of their impact on the land. Too often, western ranchers employ the "Columbus school" of grazing management: Turn the cows out in May and go discover them in October. Left alone, cattle will choose to "hang out" along streams and creeks, causing them to degrade due to excessive trampling and overgrazing. This continuous or unmanaged grazing is not a positive ecological disturbance.

By contrast, the CS, and other progressive ranches, bunch their cattle together and keep them on the move, rotating the animals frequently through numerous pastures. Ideally, under this system no single piece of ground gets grazed by cattle more than once a year, thus ensuring plenty of time for the plants to recover—which is the way nature meant for grass to be grazed. The keys are *control* of the cattle, which can be done with fencing or a herder, and *timing*, in which the herd moves are carefully planned and monitored.

In fact, as many ranchers have learned, overgrazing is much more a function of timing than numbers of cattle.

Conservationists could also learn, as I did, that much of the damage we see today on the land is historical—a legacy of the "Boom Years" of cattle grazing in the West. Between 1880 and 1920 millions of hungry animals roamed uncontrolled across the range, and the overgrazing they caused was so extensive, and so alarming, that by 1910 the U.S. government was already setting up programs to slow and heal the damage. Today, cattle numbers are down, way down, from historic highs—a fact not commonly voiced in the heat of the cattle debate.

The Davis family had done what was necessary to maintain their ethic and stay in business. New knowledge allowed them to adjust their operation to evolving values, technologies, and ideas. Rather than fight change, they had switched.

As the embers of the campfire burned softly into the night, I wondered if the conservation movement could do the same.

LAND HEALTH

My friend Dan Dagget likes to tell a story about a professor of environmental studies he knows who took a group of students for a walk in the woods near Flagstaff, Arizona. Stopping in a meadow, the professor pointed at the ground and asked, not-so-rhetorically, "Can anyone tell me if this land is healthy or not?" After a few moments of awkward silence, one student finally spoke up. "Tell us first if it's grazed by cows or not," he demanded.

Another story comes from a kayaking lawyer in Santa Fe, who told me that a workshop on land monitoring at the boundary between a working ranch and a wildlife refuge south of Albuquerque had completely rearranged his thinking. "I've done a lot of hiking and thought I knew what land health was," he said, "but when we did those transects on the ground on both sides of the fence, I saw that my ideas were all wrong."

These two instances illustrate a recurring theme in my experience as a conservationist. To paraphrase a famous quote by a Supreme Court justice, members of environmental organizations "can't define what healthy land is but they know it when they see it."

The principle problem is that we are "land illiterate." When it comes to "reading" a landscape, we might as well be studying a foreign language. Too many of us don't know our perennials from our annuals, what the signs of poor water cycling are, what an incised channel means, or, simply by looking, whether a meadow is healthy or not.

For a long time this situation wasn't our fault. What all of us lacked—rancher, conservationist, range professional, curious onlooker—was a common language to describe the common ground below our feet.

That has changed.

In 1994 the National Academy of Sciences published a book entitled *Rangeland Health: New Methods to Classify, Inventory, and Monitor Rangelands.* In it, the authors define health "as the degree to which the integrity of the soil and ecological processes of rangeland ecosystems are sustained."

They go on to say, "The capacity of rangelands to produce commodities and to satisfy values on a sustained basis depends on internal, self-sustaining ecological processes such as soil development, nutrient cycling, energy flow, and the structure and dynamics of plant and animal communities."

It is the language of soil, grass, and water.

The concept behind rangeland health is a simple but powerful one: Before land can sustainably support a value, such as livestock grazing, hunting, recreation, or wildlife protection, it must be functioning properly at a basic ecological level. In other words, before we, as a society, can talk about designating critical habitat for endangered species, or increasing forage for cows, or expanding recreational use, we need to know the answer to a simple question: Is the land healthy at the level of soil, grass, and water?

If the answer is "no," then all our values may be at risk.

Or as Kirk Gadzia, an educator, range expert, and coauthor of the book likes to put it, "It all comes down to soil. If it's stable, there's hope for the future. But if it's moving, then all bets are off for the ecosystem." It is a sentiment echoed by Roger Bowe, an award-winning rancher from eastern New Mexico, who says, "Bare soil is the rancher's number one enemy."

It must become the number one enemy of conservationists as well.

The publication of *Rangeland Health* was the touchstone for a new consensus within the scientific and range professional communities. It paved the way for the debut, in 2000, of a federal publication entitled *Interpreting*

Indicators of Rangeland Health, which provides a seventeen-point checklist for the qualitative assessment of upland health. The indicators include the presence of rills, gullies, bare ground, scouring, pedestaling, litter movement, soil compaction, plant diversity, and invasive species—the vocabulary of land health.

These were the indicators that formed the basis of the Altar Valley map that I described.

The National Riparian Team, a federal interagency team dedicated to stream health, developed a similar approach. Their seventeen-point checklist assesses the physical functioning of riparian and wetland areas through "consideration of hydrology, vegetation, and soil/landform attributes."

The goal of this assessment, which the National Riparian Team calls Proper Functioning Condition, is "to provide information on whether a riparian-wetland area is physically functioning in a manner which will allow the maintenance or recovery of desired values, e.g., fish habitat, neotropical birds, or forage, over time."

Scientists at the USDA's Jornada Experimental Range, near Las Cruces, New Mexico, recently published a peer-reviewed protocol for quantitatively measuring rangeland health, the next step after an assessment. Using a methodology that quantifies a watershed's ability to resist degradation, as well as recover from disturbance, this protocol, according to the manual, "is designed to quantify the potential of the system to function to support a range of societal values rather than to support any particular value."

Healthy land, in other words, supports many values while unhealthy land offers diminishing support over the long run.

At the risk of bending the medical metaphor too far, consider the issue this way: if it is your personal goal to run a marathon, work in a garden, write a novel, or simply survive another busy day, your ability to accomplish these goals depends on whether you are functioning properly, i.e., whether you are healthy.

That's why your doctor evaluates various standard indicators, such as pulse rate and blood pressure, when determining your relative health.

This was the message I tried to communicate to the young activist under the tree that hot summer day—that a rangeland health paradigm, employing standard indicators, allows all land to be evaluated equally and fairly. By adopting it, the conservation movement could begin to heed Aldo Leopold's advice that any activity that degrades an area's "land mechanism," as he called it, should be curtailed or changed, while any activity which maintains, restores, or expands it should be supported.

It should not matter if that activity is ranching or recreation.

CHACO

In an attempt to understand the issues of land health better, I paid a visit to a famous fenceline contrast. This particular fence separated the Navajo Nation, and its cows, from Chaco Culture National Historical Park, a World Heritage site and archaeological preserve located in the high desert of northwest New Mexico.

Cattle-free for over fifty years, Chaco's ecological condition became a pedagogical issue some years back when a controversial biologist used the boundary to highlight the dangers of too much rest from the effects of natural disturbance, including grazing and fire, in the park.

I wanted to see the fenceline contrast for myself, but I knew I would need help with the looking. So I asked Kirk Gadzia to come along.

Both of us were well aware of the park's history—that a century of overgrazing by livestock had badly degraded the land surrounding the famous ruins. We also understood that the era's typical response to this legacy of overuse was to "protect" the land from further degradation, principally with the tools of federal ownership and a barbed wire fence. It was a common, and probably appropriate, scenario played out all across the West at the time.

But Kirk and I didn't go to Chaco to argue with history or pick a fight with the National Park Service. We weren't there to offer solutions to any particular problem either. We simply wanted to take the pulse of the land on both sides of a fence.

Here's what we saw at the eastern boundary of the park: On the Chaco side we saw a great deal of bare ground, as well as many forbs, shrubs, and other woody material, some of it dead. We saw few young plants, few perennial or bunch grasses, lots of wide spaces between plants, lots of oxidized, gray plant matter, and a great deal of poor plant vigor. We saw undisturbed capped soil (bad for seed germination) and abundant evidence of soil movement, including gullies and other signs of erosion.

On the positive, we saw a greater diversity of plant species than on the Navajo side, more birds, more seed production, no sign of manure, and no sign of overgrazing.

On the Navajo side we saw lots of plant cover and litter, lots of perennial grasses, tight spaces between plants, few woody species, a wide age-class distribution among the plants, little evidence of oxidization, and lots of bunch grasses. We saw little evidence of soil movement, no gullies, and far fewer signs of erosion than on the Chaco side.

On the negative, we saw less species diversity, poor plant vigor, a great deal of compacted soil, fewer birds, less seed production, a great deal of manure, and numerous signs of overgrazing.

"So, which side is healthier?" I asked Kirk.

"Neither one is healthy, really," he replied, "not from a watershed perspective anyway." He noted that the impact of livestock grazing on the Navajo side was heavy; plants were not being given enough time to recover before being bitten again (Kirk's definition of overgrazing). As a result, the plants lacked the vigor they would have exhibited in the presence of well-managed grazing.

However, Kirk thought the Chaco side was in greater danger, primarily because it exhibited major soil instability due to gullying, capped soil, and lack of plant litter.

"The major contributing factor to this condition is the lack of tightly spaced perennial plants," he said, "which exposes the soil to the erosive effects of wind and rain. When soil loss is increased, options for the future are reduced."

"But isn't Chaco supposed to be healthier because it's protected from grazing?" I asked.

"That's what people always seem to assume," said Kirk. "In my experience in arid environments around the world, total rest from grazing has predictable results. In the first few years, there is an intense response in the system as the pressure of overgrazing is lifted. Plant vigor, diversity, and abundance often return at once and all appears to be functioning normally. Over the years, however, if the system does not receive periodic natural disturbance, by fire or grazing for example, then the overall health of the land deteriorates. And that's what we are seeing on the Chaco side."

Then Kirk put a caveat in place.

"Maybe land health isn't the issue here," he said. "It may be more about values. Is rest producing what the park wants? Ecologically, the answer is probably 'no.' But from a cultural perspective, the answer might be 'yes.' From the public perspective too. People may not want to see fire or grazing in their park."

But at what price, I wondered? Later in the day we learned that the Park Service was so worried about the threat of erosion to Chaco's world-class ruins that they intended to spend a million dollars constructing an erosion control structure in Chaco Wash. This told us the agency knows it has a "functionality" crisis on its hands.

But how can proper functioning condition be restored if the Park Service's hands are tied by a cultural value that says Chaco must be "protected" from incompatible activities, even those which might have a beneficial role to play in restoring the park to health?

As I drove home, I realized that this tension between "value" and "function" at Chaco was a sign of a new conflict spreading slowly across the West—symbolized by a fence. The cherished "protection" paradigm, embedded in the conservation movement since the days of John Muir, rubbed against something new, something energetic—something on the other side of the fence.

Untrammeled

The passage of the Wilderness Act in 1964 was a seminal event in the history of the American conservation movement. For the first time, wilderness had a legal status, enabling the process of "wildland" protection, which had been frustrated in that era of environmental exploitation, to become possible. Energized, the conservation movement grabbed the wilderness bull by both horns and has not let go to this day.

But the Act's passage also had an unforeseen consequence—it set in motion the modern struggle between value and function in our western landscapes.

This tension took a while to develop. In 1964, there was intellectual harmony between the social and ecological arguments for the creation of a federal wilderness system. No reconciliation was necessary between the Act's definition of wilderness as a tract of land "untrammeled by man ... in which man is a visitor who does not remain" and Aldo Leopold's declaration, published in *A Sand County Almanac* fifteen years earlier, that wilderness areas needed protection because they were ecological "base datums of normality."

Leopold asserted that wilderness was "important as a laboratory for the study of land health," insisting that in many cases "we literally do not know how good a performance to expect of healthy land unless we have a wild area for comparison with sick ones."

Author Wallace Stegner extended the medical metaphor when he argued that wilderness was "good for our spiritual health even if we never once in ten years set foot in it."

But a lot has changed in the years since the passage of the Wilderness Act. While most Americans still believe wilderness is necessary for social health, few ecologists now argue that wilderness areas can be considered as "base datums" of ecological health.

For example, in an article published in the journal *Wild Earth* in 2001 entitled "Would Ecological Landscape Restoration Make the Bandelier Wilderness More or Less of a Wilderness?" the authors, including ecologist Craig Allen, who has studied Bandelier National Monument, located in north-central New Mexico, for nearly twenty years, state matter-of-factly that "Most wilderness areas in the continental United States are not pristine, and ecosystem research has shown that conditions in many are deteriorating."

It is their opinion that the Bandelier Wilderness is suffering from "unnatural change," mostly as a result of historic overuse of the area, which has triggered unprecedented change in the park's ecosystems, resulting in degraded and unsustainable conditions. "Similar changes," they write, "have occurred throughout much of the Southwest."

Specifically, soils in Bandelier are "eroding at net rates of about one-half inch per decade. Given soil depths averaging only one to two feet in many areas, there will be loss of entire soil bodies across extensive areas." This is bad because the loss of topsoil, and the resulting loss of water available for plants, impedes the growth of all-important grass cover, thus reducing the incidence of natural and ecologically necessary fires.

Eliminating grazing is no panacea for Bandelier's functionality crisis, however. Herbivore exclosures established in 1975 show that protection from grazing, by itself, "fails to promote vegetative recovery," they write. Without management intervention, they argue, this human-caused case of accelerated soil erosion will become irreversible. They warn, "To a significant degree the park's biological productivity and cultural resources are literally washing away."

Their summation is provocative: "We have a choice when we know land is 'sick.' We can 'make believe,'" to quote Aldo Leopold, "that everything will turn out alright if Nature is left to take its course in our unhealthy wildernesses, or we can intervene—adaptively and with humility—to facilitate the healing process."

This turns a great deal of conservation thinking on its head.

Wallace Stegner once wrote, "Wildlife sanctuaries, national seashores and lakeshores, wild and scenic rivers, wilderness areas created under the 1964 Wilderness Act, all represent a strengthening of the decision to hold onto land and manage large sections of the public domain rather than dispose of them *or let them deteriorate*." [emphasis added]

But we have let them deteriorate—as the Buenos Aires, Chaco, and

Bandelier examples demonstrate. Whether their deteriorated condition is a result of historical overuse or some more recent activity is not as important as another question: What are we going to do to heal land we know to be sick?

Clearly it's not 1964, or 1946, anymore. The harmony between value and function in the landscape, including our "protected" places, has deteriorated along with the topsoil.

This functionality crisis raises important questions for the conservation community. What, for instance, are the long-term prospects for wildlife populations in the West, including keystone predator species, if the ecological integrity of these special places is being compromised at the level of soil, grass, and water?

Can land be truly "wild" if it is not functioning properly?

Also, does "protection" from human activity preclude intervention, and if so, at what cost to ecosystem health? And on a larger scale, how do we "protect" our parks and wildernesses from the effects of global warming, acid rain, and noxious weed invasion?

And what about private land? Half of the American West is privately owned. What does a newly sprouted housing subdivision indicate about the long-term prospects for the health of the land as a whole?

HEALING

The arguments and conditions that paved the way for a national wilderness system, as well as for the expansion of other "protected" areas, including new national parks and wildlife refuges, seem anachronistic today.

It should be clear by now that drawing lines on a map in order to shield chunks of land from threats posed by certain types of human activity without simultaneously confronting the source of those threats in the first place—the way we live as a society—is "fixing the pump without fixing the well," as Leopold put it.

Additionally, the whole concept of "preserving" some places while "sacrificing" others creates a stratification of land quality and land use that is harmful to land health because it doesn't treat land holistically.

As conservationist Charles Little has written, "Leopold insisted on dealing with land whole: the system of soils, waters, animals, and plants that make up a community called 'the land.' But we insist on discriminating. We apply our money and our energy in behalf of protection on a selective basis."

He goes on to say, "The idea of a hierarchy in land quality is *the* tenet of the conservation and environmental movement."

Since John Muir's day, the conservation movement has based this hierarchy on the concept of "pristineness"—the degree to which an area of land remains untrammeled by humans. As late as 1964, before the maturation of ecology as a discipline, it was still possible to believe in the pristine quality of wilderness as an ecological fact, as Leopold did. Today, however, pristineness must be acknowledged to be a value, something that exists mostly in the eye of the beholder.

Biologist Peter Raven puts it in blunt ecological terms: "There is not a square centimeter anywhere on earth, whether it is in the middle of the Amazon basin or the center of the Greenland ice cap, that does not receive every minute some molecules of a substance made by human beings."

Pristineness can no longer be the bottom line of the conservation movement. In fact, the word should be deleted from the movement's vocabulary.

Many conservation professionals understand this, which is one reason why in recent years there has been a strong movement toward biodiversity as a more appropriate bottom line. This is an important and hopeful development, especially since it is strongly science-based. Unfortunately, much of this work still rests on the preservation/protection model, which means it is still hierarchical and exclusionary.

For example, a recent major land acquisition campaign by the Nature Conservancy, the largest conservation organization in the nation, urged its members to help it save "The Last Best Places" in the country (provoking the iconoclast in me to want to direct a campaign titled "What About the Rest of the West?").

When money and time are short, as they chronically are, this discriminatory approach is pragmatic, especially if biodiversity is under imminent threat. Ultimately, however, it strikes me as still doing more for the pump than for the well.

I believe the new bottom line must be *land health*. By assessing all types of land equally, a land health paradigm enforces an egalitarian approach to land quality, thereby reducing conflicts caused by clashing cultural values. By giving us a target of ecological functionality, it also enables land owners and managers to prioritize their restoration work, if restoration work is required. And by employing a common set of indicators, it creates a road map for living sustainably on the land—starting at the level of soil, grass, and water.

For example, there is a chunk of Bureau of Land Management (BLM) land west of Taos, New Mexico, that will never be a wilderness area, national park, or wildlife refuge. It is modest land, mostly flat, covered with sage, and very dry. In its modesty, however, it is typical of millions of acres of public land across the West.

It is typical in another way too—it exists in a degraded ecological condition, the result of historic overgrazing and modern neglect. A recent qualitative land health assessment revealed its poor condition in stark terms, confronting the BLM with the knowledge that more than forty years of total rest from livestock grazing had not healed the land. Some of it, in fact, teetered on an ecological threshold, threatening to transition to a deeper degraded state.

Fortunately, as humble and unhealthy as this land is, it is not unloved. The wildlife like it, of course, but so do the owners of the private land intermingled with the BLM land, some of whom built homes there. The area's two new ranchers also have great affection for this unassuming land and want to see it healed.

These ranchers are using cattle as agents of ecological restoration. Through the effect of carefully controlled herding, they intend to trample the sage and bare soil, much of which is capped solid, so that native grasses can get reestablished again. The ranchers are calling this act of restoration a "Poop-and-Stomp," and its effects are being carefully monitored using the new land health protocols.

Using cattle to restore rangelands is not as crazy as it sounds. In fact, in his 1933 classic book *Game Management*, Aldo Leopold wrote that wildlife "can be restored with the same tools that have hithertofore destroyed it: fire, ax, cow, gun, and plow." The difference, of course, is the management of the tool, as well as the goals of the tool user.

Another example of "using nature to heal nature" is the work of Bill Zeedyk, who uses the power of small flood events to restore degraded streams to health. Called "Induced Meandering," Bill's approach is to place simple wood-and-rock structures at carefully calibrated points in incised stream channels so when the flood event comes the water is diverted into the opposite stream bank, thus "remeandering" the channel, which dissipates energy and encourages riparian vegetation to take hold and grow. Bill calls this innovative, yet humble, restoration strategy "thinking like a creek."

Both the Taos project and Bill Zeedyk's efforts are emblematic of a new conservation approach in the West. *In fact, I am convinced that land health and restoration, not wilderness and protection, will become the principle paradigms of a new conservation movement in the not-so-distant future.* Our goal will be a thousand acts of restoration, which I define as achieving full ecological functionality at the level of soil, grass, and water.

Our job as conservationists will be to transform red to green on maps such as that of the Altar Valley, and to do so collaboratively—for without local support (and maintenance) most restoration work will be jeopardized in the long run.

SOCIAL HEALTH

If I could wave a magic wand across the American West and instantaneously produce a land health map for the whole region, I think all of us—rancher, conservationist, scientist, private land owner, public land manager, and public land owner (you)—would be shocked by what we would see.

I have little doubt that we would see a map dominated by reds and oranges across wide stretches, with isolated stretches of deep and pale greens. The reasons for the dominance of reds and oranges across this map would be multiple, widely varied, and often site specific—as would potential restoration strategies.

However, this "land sickness," as Leopold called it, is not the only illness afflicting the rural West. Depressed economies, governmental gridlock, cultural clashes, demographic pressures, political disenfranchisement, and a host of other maladies have descended in force on rural counties, contributing in large measure to the frustration and anger that characterize so much of the region today.

In other words, social health in the West is in as much need of restoration as the physical landscape.

A big step toward restoring both would be to create an economic incentive to restoring land to functionality. The other parts of the puzzle are in place—the restoration toolbox is well developed, as is the scientific understanding of ecological processes that can guide restoration work. We certainly don't know everything, but as ecologist and restoration advocate Craig Allen likes to say, "we know enough now to get started."

And who better to do the job than people with local knowledge and great affection for local land? Long-term, meaningful restoration cannot be accomplished long-distance by well-meaning urban volunteers—the job is too big and too complex. Curing what ails western land will require local doctors, local remedies, local elbow grease—and local paychecks.

The good news is the labor pool is already in place. Ranch families are spread out across the West—at least for the time being.

Additionally, the compensation of ranchers and other rural landowners for producing ecological services to society, in the form of cleaner and more abundant water in these dry times for instance, will become an increasingly important economic engine in the not-so-distant future.

But that's another topic. The issue here is how the conservation movement will adjust to meet, and support, these emerging trends. The adoption of a land health paradigm is the first step, but the concomitant question of who does the restoration, and how they get paid, requires another major realignment of the movement's philosophy.

If going back to school means reexamining the concept of pristineness, it also means reexamining its historical antithesis—work.

Under the old wilderness paradigm, conservationists traditionally segregated work from nature, thereby creating, according to historian Richard White, "a set of dualisms where work can only mean the absence of nature and nature can only mean human leisure."

White argues that conservationists need to reexamine work or else condemn ourselves to spending most of our lives outside of nature. "Having demonized those whose very lives recognize the tangled complexity of a planet in which we kill, destroy and alter as a condition of living and working," he writes, "we can claim an innocence that in the end is merely irresponsibility."

If the conservation movement could instead focus on work rather than on leisure, White says, then a whole new approach is possible. Focusing on work "links us to each other, and it links us to nature," he writes. "It unites issues as diverse as workplace safety and grazing on public lands; it unites toxic sites and wilderness areas. In taking responsibility for our own lives and work, in unmasking the connections of our labor and nature, in giving up our hopeless fixation on purity, we may ultimately find a way to break the borders that imprison nature as much as ourselves. Work, then, is where we should begin."

Again, we must start with a land health paradigm. Not only does it address the functionality crisis confronting the West, but it also can help chart a path through the region's value crisis as well. Qualitative and quantitative assessments of land health can create a baseline of fact that can guide our fancy, potentially helping us to resolve some of the destructive cultural clashes and dualisms that plague the region—jobs vs. the environment, urban vs. rural, work vs. play—clashes that are undermining our common goal of creating "a society to match its scenery," as Wallace Stegner once lamented.

Equally important, by directing restoration work and encouraging the

economic activity that goes with it, a land health paradigm can help restore
social function to communities and economies in the West.

By developing a common language to describe the common ground
below our feet, by working collaboratively to heal land and restore rural
economies, by monitoring our progress scientifically, and by linking function to value in a constructive manner, a land health paradigm can steer us
toward fulfilling Stegner's dream.

The Working Wilderness

Not long ago I had the privilege of riding a horse into the West Elks Wilderness, high in the mountains above Paonia, Colorado. I wanted to see an
award-winning cattle-herding operation in action and to learn more about
the compatibility between well-managed ranching and wilderness values.

I also wanted to see some pretty country.

So did Steve Allen, who moved his family to Paonia in the early 1970s as
part of that era's "back-to-the-land" movement. Switching from farming
to ranching in the late 1980s, he went back to school to learn the principles
of progressive cattle management. Upon his return he convinced five other
ranchers with permits in the West Elks to form a pool and begin herding
their cattle as one unit through the mountains. They also convinced the
Forest Service to let them give it a try.

Today, pool riders guide the thousand-head herd of cattle through a long
arc in the mountains with the aid of border collies and the occasional temporary electric fence. They move the herd every ten days or so, which allows
the land plenty of time to recover; and since traditional fences are no longer
necessary, the ranchers voluntarily removed hundreds of miles of barbed
wire fence in the wilderness, a boon to wildlife and backpackers alike.

In addition, Steve employs a new method of low-stress livestock han-
dling whose gentleness would make John Wayne roll his eyes.

The local Forest Service range conservationist, Dave Bradford, went
to school too and came back determined to quantify the effects of this
new thinking. He rides the range frequently, reads monitoring transects

constantly, and publishes the results. He has also done quite a bit of historical research, including uncovering "before" photographs of the range, in order to gain new knowledge on the conditions of the land.

Steve and Dave were my hosts for the day, and I was as eager to see the evidence of their labors as they were to show it off.

I couldn't resist an act of bridge-building, though, so I brought along the new director of a Paonia-based conservation organization. The support of her predecessor for the West Elks herding experiment had been crucial to its early success, and I was curious about what she thought as an heir to the project. I also knew she had recently backpacked the very trail we were riding that morning.

What we saw shocked us at first. The herd of cattle had moved along the trail just days before, beating it into a muddy pulp. It looked like a tornado had touched down; shattered brush and trampled grass were ubiquitous, as was the cow poop. It certainly was not your standard Sierra Club calendar image of wilderness.

"This looks great!" yelled Dave as we climbed a steep hill on horseback. "Look at all this disturbance. Come back here in a month and you would never know the cattle went through here, it'll be so lush."

I turned to the director of the conservation organization.

"People call me all the time and complain," she said. "They're hikers. They don't think there should be cows in the wilderness."

"What do you tell them?" I asked.

"I tell them it's a working wilderness," she replied, spurring her horse forward.

Steve led us to a high meadow where we found a small bunch of cattle that had broken off from the main herd. After lunch we spent the rest of the day driving the cattle back down the mountain in a chaotic rush of snapping branches, surging adrenaline, and hard work. It was Steve's sly way—I realized when we reached the bottom of the mountain, exhausted and exhilarated—of teaching us a lesson about values.

Before our education began, however, we all sat in the green meadow and ate lunch among the blooming wildflowers, admiring the view. Each of us—rancher, federal manager, and activist—shared the same thought: What a treasure this land is! Sitting there, I was reminded of why I became a conservationist—to explore the solace of open spaces; to look and learn, and teach in turn; to celebrate cultural diversity alongside biological diversity; and to revel in nature's model of good health.

And to try to understand, as John Muir did, that every part of the universe is hitched to everything else.